Presented to:

Presented by:

Date:

The Divine Stories of the Yahweh Sisterhood

ISBN: 1-880809-42-7
Printed in the United States of America

Legacy Publishers International
1301 South Clinton Street
Denver, CO 80247
www.legacypublishersinternational.com

1 2 3 4 5 6 7 8 9 10 11 / 09 08 07 06

The Divine Stories of the Yahweh Sisterhood

by

Michelle Medlock Adams

and

Gena Maselli

Dedication

I dedicate this book to my mother, Marion Medlock.

You have always been my closest friend, my biggest fan, my spiritual mentor, and the best mother a girl could ever dream of. For all of those reasons and so many more, I dedicate this book to you.

Michelle Medlock Adams

I dedicate this book to my mother, Patricia Pfeifer Heinen, for sharing her faith, her life, and her wisdom.

Gena Maselli

Table of Contents

Introduction

When Michelle and Gena first came up with the idea for *The Divine Stories of the Yahweh Sisterhood,* they weren't sure what the final results would bring. Michelle had thought of the title for the book while at a writers' conference in June 2002. She knew she wanted to create a book celebrating Sisterhood in Christ using that title, but doing the project alone just didn't seem right. So, she called Gena to ask if she would consider co-authoring the book with her. What better way to celebrate Sisterhood in Christ than to write the book with a friend? After talking it through, Gena suggested making it a compilation book, allowing women from around the world to share their Christian sisters in their own words.

And so their journey began.

Of course, making the decision to undertake the co-authoring of a book isn't a light one. Michelle and Gena discussed and prayerfully considered whether their friendship would be strong enough to weather the intricate process—story selections; deadlines; melding styles, edits, and re-edits. Thankfully, not only has their friendship survived, it's thrived!

"Through creating the *Yahweh Sisterhood* book, Michelle and I have become the forever kind of friends and sisters in faith that our book promotes," Gena says without hesitation. "I couldn't think of anyone I'd rather work with. It's so nice to know that, not only am I working with someone so talented, but when things get stressful, I also have a good friend, who can say, 'Don't let it get you down. Just get a Snickers and a Coke and keep going.'"

Michelle agrees.

"This journey wouldn't have been as meaningful or as special if I hadn't walked it with Gena," she shares. "When I moved to Texas, leaving behind my best friends in Indiana, I longed for a best buddy in my new surroundings. I was tired of being alone in the Lone Star State. I am so happy that God answered my prayer for a close friend with Gena. She's everything a friend should be—not to mention a very gifted writer."

Of course, all relationships take work—even sisters in Christ.

During the writing process, Michelle and Gena both experienced challenges in their relationships with other women—friends, peers, and family.

"It was like some sort of test or joke. At the point when we were writing about the greatness of Sisterhood in Christ, we sometimes felt so unqualified to write about it," Gena admits. "Some days I jokingly turned to Michelle and said, 'But I don't think I like women today!'"

Of course, those were the days when Michelle laughed and answered, offering the emergency Snickers and Coke pick-me-up combo, "I know, but that's how we know God's going to use this book, because it'll be in spite of us and not because of us."

So, as you enjoy the powerful, and sometimes tearful, stories in *The Divine Stories of the Yahweh Sisterhood,* Michelle and Gena hope God will remind you—just as He did them during the writing of the book—that Sisterhood in Christ really is a heavenly gift. It's to be celebrated, cherished, shared, and passed on. They hope that after reading this book, you'll be prompted to take a minute from your busy schedule, call a girlfriend or two, and treasure your time—together.

How to Use This Book

It is our desire that *The Divine Stories of the Yahweh Sisterhood* will not only be an entertaining read for you, but also a spiritual journey toward a closer relationship with God and the special women in your life.

For that reason, we have created additional godly goodies for you at the end of each chapter. You certainly don't have to partake in these "extra servings," but we hope you will want to dig in!

Intimate Details:

This section highlights biblical passages that relate to the subject matter within that chapter. These can be used as memory verses, or simply as faith-builders.

Heart to Heart:

We developed this section with small groups and Bible study buddies in mind. This section offers thought-provoking discussion questions that will cause you to look into your heart and mind, asking the sometimes difficult questions.

Up Close and Personal:

If you're a journaler, you'll love this bonus section. Our questions and suggestions are meant to awaken the writer in each of you. There is much healing that takes place through writing, so we hope you'll take the time to journal your deepest hopes, thoughts, and dreams—either in the space provided or in your own personal journal.

Inspirational Insight:

We want each chapter to leave you with a nugget of wisdom and truth—something you can mentally chew on for a while. This isn't meant to be a "preachy" section; rather it's designed to further drive home the point of the chapter and challenge you in your faith and relationships.

Celebrate the Moment:

After we've challenged you, we want to take all of that enthusiasm and renewed spirit and use it to bless someone else—mainly a Yahweh sister. While we suggest simple gestures such as sending an "I'm-thinking-of-you-today" card, you can take our ideas and make them your own—using your own creativity and personality to really celebrate the sisters in your life.

Heart to Heaven:

We couldn't think of a better way to end each chapter than to pray with you. Even though we can't be in the same room with you, our hearts are there with you as you pray the simple prayer in each Heart to Heaven section. These prayers are meant to open a line of communication between you and your heavenly Father. We hope they are just a starting point, and that you'll take each prayer in whatever direction the Father leads you to take.

❧ ❧ ❧

Although we can't physically be with you as you take this Yahweh Sisterhood journey, we are there with you in spirit. Every story, every insight, every word was prayed over and put together with you in mind. We feel very connected to you. After all, we're Yahweh sisters! Now, enjoy the journey …

Chapter One

GIRLFRIEND GET-TOGETHERS:

Taking Time to Share Laughter and Life

Where two or three are gathered together in my name, there am I in the midst of them.

Matthew 18:20 KJV

Have you ever taken your girlfriends for granted? Have you ever rushed through your life folding laundry, running a car pool, and keeping the immaculate daily planner instead of investing in your friends? It's easy to do. It's easy to get caught up in checking items off our to-do lists instead of making a deposit in others' lives or allowing them to deposit into ours.

This became so real to me a few years ago when during a seminar, I was asked to list the ten most important things in my life. In my handy, and yes, immaculate daily planner, I rattled ten things off the top of my head: God, family, health, friends, etc. There was nothing extraordinary on my list. Honestly, it was probably similar to everyone else's. But then the speaker asked me to rank them. That's when I realized my friends came very close to the top of my list. As I sat there half-listening to the speaker talk about life goals, I wondered when I'd last invested in my friendships—and I mean more than a mere "how ya doin'" before church or a witty e-mail forward. Honestly, I couldn't remember. Instead, I remembered the times I'd passed up getting together because I was "too busy." I realized I'd missed some great memories because I was consumed with checking items off my to-do list.

Of course, when those *eurekas* hit you, you can't wallow in self-pity or feel condemned. No, the best you can do is begin anew. Start where you are and make time for your friends. Even if you're not a gifted party-planner who can pull off the ideal *Anne of Green Gables* brunch, don't get discouraged. You can still plan a Girlfriend Get-Together. Trust me; showing up is half the battle. *GM*

We'll Always Have Starbucks

Gena Maselli

"So, how's work? Anyone implode under the pressure yet?" Lisa jokingly asked. Her quizzical eyes searched me for the truth about how tough things really were.

"No, but the week's not over yet," I answered flippantly.

"Isn't it any better since they started making changes?" Camille wondered, shaking her head in sad amazement.

I hesitated, trying to think of the best answer.

Julie suddenly spoke up. "Everyone's just waiting and praying, hoping for the best."

All of us knew the struggles of the workplace. We'd been with our company long enough to see many highs and lows—maybe *too* many. As with many organizations, change was in the air. Though Lisa and Camille had left to be at-home-mothers, they still felt connected. Julie and I, on the other hand, continued to forge our way in the company—in the midst of restructuring and speculated layoffs. Thank God the four of us had each other to keep one another sane. What started as meetings over dinner to celebrate birthdays and promotions turned into monthly "get-away-from-everything" retreats at the local Starbucks.

Each time we meet, we confiscate the most comfortable overstuffed chairs in the place. Pulling them into a circle, we huddle, breathe in the fresh roasted aromas, listen to jazzy melodies, and exchange the latest in our lives. No husbands; no children. It's *our* time to update, encourage, and completely enjoy ourselves. And because of it, we are no longer mere workplace acquaintances. We are friends, chosen sisters.

Every time we meet, I look around and feel such a privilege to be a part of this group. They were an answer to my frantic prayers. There was a time when I was new in town, fresh out of college, newly married, and desperately praying for friends like the ones I had left behind. Though each of us is unique, we share a common thread that binds us more than the most endearing character trait—our faith. No matter what direction we move, we all begin at the same point. Our talents and flaws differ, but our decision and need to approach our lives from a spiritually biblical base never wavers. And this, more than anything else in our lives, holds our friendship together.

> Our talents and flaws differ, but our decision and need to approach our lives from a spiritually biblical base never wavers. And this, more than anything else in our lives, holds our friendship together.
>
> —Gena Maselli

In a day when busyness overwhelms even the most even-tempered person, to the point that many of us don't even know our closest neighbors, having girlfriends who share my faith is a gift. I may not even talk to them much in between our getaways, but I'm confident that when we meet, we'll pick up right where we left off and catch up on each others' lives.

Over the years, we've walked through births, deaths, job changes, cross-country moves, church splits, diets, and garage sales. And through all the good and the bad, we've experienced God's abundant grace in our own lives and the lives of our loved ones. We've sought His direction, enjoyed His forgiveness, and gratefully accepted His healing—together.

I'm not naïve. I know that one day this group will change. One of us may move away or change schedules, making it impossible to meet. And when that time comes, I hope that each of us will look for other like-minded, faith-based friends to share in our lives. I believe we will because we've known the benefit of it.

But for now, as we look to the near future and see more children, home purchases, and birthdays, we'll continue to meet at Starbucks, hogging the most comfy chairs in the place. Over steaming cups of soothing Chai tea, we'll continue to celebrate the big and the small events in our lives.

Gena Maselli is a freelance writer who lives in Fort Worth, Texas, with her husband children's author Christopher P.N. Maselli, their daughter and two feline friends. She is the author and co-author of several books, including *Daily Wisdom for Working Women*, *Truth Unplugged for Girls* and *Truth Unplugged and Guys.*

Unparties

Raelene Phillips

"What do you do there?" is the question asked by the children and husbands of the ladies who meet periodically for UNparties. The original seven women understand, but explanation falls short. Perhaps it is best experienced. And so, yesterday, a novice was admitted. She is nineteen and the daughter of the youngest original member. She is, therefore, my third cousin.

Thirty years ago, Tupperware parties and Stanley parties were in vogue. Since we rarely saw each other, the women in my family discovered that at these parties, we did not want to listen to the "dealer" do her demonstration. We just wanted to get caught up on each others' lives. Thus, the birth of the UNparty—a gathering that is not for anything special, except to visit with our cousins and aunts.

Thirty years later, we still love these gatherings. In fact, there seems to be an urgency in all of us to have them more often. We are all aging. We realize that someday we will be missing a member of our cast.

The nineteen-year-old sat in awe.

Her grandmother, a new widow, described in hilarious detail her experience in replacing a toilet seat. We laughed till we cried when she described the years of corrosion that had "cemented" the bolts to the toilet and how her steak knife didn't really help. My mother, the matriarch of the clan at age 85, expressed thanks that in her retirement community the maintenance people would have done this. Mom's niece (who is 82) asked why she didn't have one of her sons-in-law do it. My generation wondered amidst the laughter if we would even *try* to do small home repairs without our husbands. The youngster laughed with the rest of us, but you could tell she was thinking, *What's the big deal?* (She is a sales clerk at a tractor supply store. If her work boots were any evidence, she could probably install an entire toilet, not just a seat!)

As my cousin continued with her story, we UNparty veterans nodded and said "Did you ever?"—"Well, I never!"—"Well, I never, neither!"—"Oh gosh neds!"—"Forevermore!"

The nineteen-year-old looked perplexed. Her generation knows nothing of sympathetic listening noises. They never shake their heads and "tsk" to show you that they understand. Often it is hard to know if they are listening at all. It is the difference between those who stare straight ahead with a bored expression in a church service and those who say an occasional "Amen."

> UNparties are about more than just fun. They are learning in its purest form one generation of women teaching another.
>
> —Raelene Phillips

UNparties are about more than just fun. They are learning in its purest form...one generation of women teaching another. It is the *Ya Ya Sisterhood* (minus the profanity and alcohol). It is *Steel Magnolias* (minus the beauty shop). It is, for better or worse, my family! We have learned such valuable things: how long boiled eggs have to be in beet juice for them to pickle, the only way to get just the right flavor in deviled eggs (Hellmann's Real Mayonnaise—not the fat-free kind!), how to housebreak a puppy, and how to survive the loss of a spouse. Our topics of conversation flow freely. We are not always all on the same page. There can be laughter on the couch and tears in the sun porch all happening at the same time. There is a certain amount of male-bashing. There is pride in children's accomplishments. There is sadness over divorce. Since we all share the same faith, there are always some scriptural insights gained.

By the end of the party, (which *always* runs from 9 a.m. to 3 p.m.—so the husband of the house will know when he can safely come home), the nineteen-year-old had joined in with anecdotes of her own. As my half-blind mother told of her problems seeing at a recent candlelit dinner, my young third cousin looked at me and disgustedly uttered, "Did you ever?"

Another generation of UNpartiers has come.

Raelene Phillips is a speaker and author of *The Freedom Trilogy,* a trilogy of historical Christian fiction. Her essay on faith received honorable mention in a contest by Obadiah Press. It will be printed in the anthology, *Living by Faith.* She is a graduate of CLASS (Christian Leaders, Authors, and Speakers Services) seminar.

Heart to Heart:

When was the last time you had a Girlfriend Get-Together?

Describe the experience—the people, the setting, the event.

What made it special to you?

The Bus-Stop Mommies

Karen Rinehart

You can learn a lot about life from standing at the bus stop. In particular I am talking about my children's school bus stop here in my North Carolina neighborhood; but wherever you have mothers with children, you will have Bus-Stop Mommies.

We moved to Concord last February, more than halfway through the academic and school bus year. At our school in Florida, there was no bus system, so I took our lives in my hands and maneuvered the drop-off and pick-up lines every morning and afternoon. Long before I had children, I watched the school parking lot scene in the movie *Mr. Mom*, and haughtily concluded that no mother in a school parking lot could possibly be that rude.

Then I had children of my own. When I stand before the judgment throne in heaven, I am sure there will be a separate and infinitely long line specifically for Parental Parking Lot Sins. God knows I've witnessed and participated in more than I care to admit—"Hey, you moron! Could you drive a little *faster* around all these little kids?"

"So, Karen, I see your husband picked up the kids yesterday." "Why yes, I was home sick in bed. How did you know it was him?" "He was in the wrong line…you need to talk to him about that." HONK HONK HONK "Oh, pardon me, was I in the way of your big truck or was it your big ego?"

Then there was umbrella-toting Sister Maria manning the lot like Schwartzkopf with his tanks. You knew you had "arrived" when Sister reprimanded you for leaving your car in the pick-up lane unattended or nabbed you chatting with the van in the adjoining lane, thereby stalling the forward progress of the pick-up line. Let's face it, parking lots can bring out the worst in all of us, plus send a horrendous message to our little wide-eyed, sponges-for-brains children in the backseat.

That said, you can imagine my great joy of leaving behind parking-lot rage and racked-up minivan mileage. Except on the first day. Then I was just plain nervous watching my child climb aboard that big orange thing on wheels with a stranger for a driver and no seat belts in sight.

> The Bus-Stop Mommies always know where and when the next Tupperware, Pampered Chef, Bunco, and birthday party will occur. We are never more than a house away from a prayer request, borrowed egg, or wallpaper scraper.
>
> —Karen Rinehard

Anyhow, last February, the weather was cold and wet, so none of my new neighbors were outside to accost, um, I mean, introduce myself to. I was desperate to feel like I belonged in this tight-knit 'hood and especially anxious to meet the other moms. For a reason that escapes me now (big surprise there), my husband walked our daughter up to the bus stop that first anxious morning.

From my front door, I pressed my nose on the cold glass and after wiping off the fog and grime, saw them gathered around the bus stop at the top of my street....yes! They're there! All my future friends and fellow vessels of homework and hormone wisdom—oh, how I longed to *belong*.

Ahhh, the bus stop. A true suburban bevy of sleepy-eyed, mumbling, bed-headed creatures. And the children aren't always so perky, either. Last year we stumbled out of the house for the short romp up the cul-de-sac at 7:25 a.m. Most of the kids were there or tearing out their doors at the last minute. No problem. This year we have to tear out the door, toast in hand, at 7:12 or we *are* toast.

Usually no more than three kids make it on board each morning. They're still trying to get their mothers out of bed. But all eleven make the ride home in the afternoon. You see, our driver, Gloria, has won "Bus Driver of the Month" every month since school opened this year. Translated: She is never late. As a matter of fact, she is typically early. She even smiles in the morning and has the heat on for the kids during the winter. She is still smiling in the afternoon—a far better person than me, she gets to skip that long line in heaven; I am certain of it.

The Bus-Stop Mommies agree with me. We tend to agree on a lot of things because we discuss all of life's crucial topics—who has the best prices on milk, what time the mailman comes, who needs to bag their grass clippings, fourth-grade writing tests, which teachers were meant to become prison wardens, which laundry-stain fighter is the best, how to remove moldy shower caulk, and of course, anything related to the male species.

The Bus-Stop Mommies always know where and when the next Tupperware, Pampered Chef, Bunco, and birthday party will occur. We are never more than a house away from a prayer request, borrowed egg, or wallpaper scraper. Within their ranks, I have found women who share my faith, doctor, and distaste for ironing. All things wise and wonderful…they are mouthed at the Bus Stop. The Secret of Life…learned at the Bus Stop. The Be All and End All…you guessed it, at the Bus Stop.

So, the next time you need a walking buddy, a third opinion on the color of yellow you just finished painting your kitchen, moral support, or just some mommy-venting time, head to the bus stop. Call one of the gals and have her meet you there early. Therein lies your answer.

Karen Rinehart lives with her husband, two children, and one goofy dog in Concord, North Carolina. Karen writes a biweekly humor column, *True to Life*, for the *Independent Tribune* newspaper. Her works have appeared in the *Tampa Tribune*, *Canticle Magazine*, and *FlightHumor.org*. *The Bus-Stop Mommies* is a registered trademark.

Manicures, Movies and Other Nice Things

Shannon Kubiak

It had been a long Friday, and an awful week. Exhausted, I couldn't even think straight, and I was very near tears. I was glad to be leaving work, but I wasn't quite ready to go home. So I called Amy. I dialed her on my cell as I pulled out of the parking lot and she answered as she always does. "Hi, Princess," she said. "How was your day?" Her voice was cheery although I knew her week had made her just as crazy as mine had made me.

"Long," I answered and she gave both her condolences and her understanding as I proceeded to tell her about it. Amy and I were two of the busiest people I knew, and we were wearing ourselves to the bone. If anyone understood the chaos that had become my life, Amy did.

As I drove and talked, I had an epiphany. "Let's go get a manicure," I blurted out, cutting her off and almost slamming into the little blue Nissan in front of me.

Amy paused. "Really?" she asked with excitement in her voice.

"Yeah," I answered, trying to convince myself that I could actually do something nice just for me. All I had done all week was give, give, give and work, work, work, and I was ready to snap, snap, snap. Amy's week had played out the same way.

So I swung by and picked her up, and we treated ourselves to a well-deserved reward. We even got carried away and bought new lotion at Bath and Body Works. It was a "pamper-the-princesses" moment, and the worry lines and dark circles vanished from our faces momentarily.

A little over an hour later, as we walked out of the nail salon admiring our hands, Amy said something I will never forget. "We should do this more often—like every week. It has been so long since I have done anything nice for myself." "Me, too," I said sighing. Then it hit us both at the same time. In that moment we mandated a new rule. A Shannon and Amy rule. A "how-to-keep-your-sanity-in-the-midst-of-an-insane-life" rule, and we have stuck to it ever since.

We decided that each week we had to do something nice for ourselves. The size of our indulgence didn't matter, as long as we did it. Each Friday we had to report back to each other as a form of accountability. It would be our way of appreciating the little things in life—stopping to smell the roses, so to speak.

So each week Amy and I e-mailed or called each other to inquire about what the other had done for the unpampered princess inside of her. Some weeks it was small things like putting cucumbers on our eyelids for fifteen minutes, or taking a half-hour nap instead of busying ourselves with something that could wait until later to get done. Other weeks it was a bigger thing like a new pair of shoes or going to a movie. Sometimes it was even another manicure.

But each week, as I hurried through my busy life, I thought of Amy and knew that, come Friday, she would ask me what I had done for myself. As stupid, or as selfish, as our ritual may sound, it was our saving grace. It deepened our friendship, and it tangibly helped us hang on to the life that quickly passed us by.

Amy's friendship gave me something I could have never given myself—a way to relax and unwind and find my way back into God's presence in the midst of a busy week. Sometimes the time I took to hold up my end of the bargain was the only time I got to sit still all week. Amy's accountability was the greatest thing God could have given me at that time in my life. We were kindred spirits—busy spirits. And by every Friday we were joyful and refreshed spirits because of a deal that became a bond on a crazy awful Friday in a nail salon not too far from here.

Shannon Kubiak is the author of *The Divine Dance,* a book for young women on how to live for the Lord instead of performing for the world. She has a passion for God and a passion for encouraging women to know Him better. She has a BA in journalism from Biola University.

Up Close and Personal:

What is your idea of the perfect Girlfriend Get-Together?

Who would you invite?

What would you do?

What's stopping you from actually doing it?

Time With a Friend

Judith Erl

We sit surrounded by words,
Shelves upon shelves
Of words.
Our conversation seems to compete
With all this communication.

I see sitting across from me a smile
That I should see more of,
The subtle wrinkles around
Her eyes more pronounced,
Her teeth showing in laughter.

Our conversation seems, at times
Too irreverent for
These surroundings,
The conversation of
Friends,
The slang of
Silliness.

This communication is something
Very important,
Not for the
Words it contains,
Not for the thoughts
Expressed,
But good for the soul.

Judith Erl is a poet/at-home mom. Christopher, 12, and Andrea, 9, have been the inspiration for most of her children's stories with the humor and activity they bring to family life. Judith has been published in on-line publications, including *Freelancers Online* "Concentric" and "Three Cup Morning."

Celebrate the Moment:

Within the next week, plan a get-together with one or more girlfriends. It doesn't have to be expensive, time-consuming, or labor-intensive. It can be as simple as sharing peanut-butter-and-jelly sandwiches at your home or coffee after work. The important thing is to take time to nurture friendships and refresh yourself.

The Birthday Club

by Deb Kalmbach

"We call ourselves the Birthday Club," I explained to the innkeeper while lugging my suitcase into the bright yellow Victorian for the weekend.

She smiled. "It's great that you take time to get together—especially when you all live far away. You must be special friends."

"Oh, we are," I said. *If only she knew...*but how could I begin to describe the friendships forged through the many ups and downs of more than twenty years? Our little circle of five friends had grown way beyond simply celebrating our almost-mutual birthdays in August and September. We had become sisters, the kind that sticks closer than family members.

It all started when Mary (whose birthday is three days after mine) and I celebrated our birthdays at the local deli. We always exchanged small gifts and shed a few tears. Back then, our husbands both struggled with drinking problems—and often forgot us on our birthdays.

I assured Mary. "It's OK, I love and appreciate you."

"Look at us," Mary observed. "The highlight of our day is celebrating at the *Piggly Wiggly* deli!"

We laughed through our tears, hugged each other, and returned to our celebration-less homes.

Our deli party became an annual event. Our self-pity gradually changed to include prayer. We asked the Lord to help us learn contentment in our circumstances, and to focus on what was right in our marriages. To our surprise, our lists kept growing.

Connie joined our party after I met her at an office potluck where our husbands both worked. She had the all-important late August birthday—and the challenge of a difficult marriage. Connie discovered a Christ-centered support group for women called *One Step Further.* I drove to her house every Monday night and we attended the meeting together. Sometimes we sat in the car, talking, crying, and praying for what seemed like hours. We read and memorized scriptures and determined that with God's help, we would take a stand for our marriages. Now there were three of us celebrating at the *Piggly Wiggly.*

When I met Judy at church one Sunday morning, I felt as if I had known her forever. Of course, Judy's birthday arrived at the end of August, and she fit right into the Birthday Club. Judy joined us in her desire to present a more Christ-like attitude to her husband. I often called her when my sagging attitude needed her optimism.

She encouraged me in her soft-spoken way. "Call me anytime you need to talk, Deb. I don't have all the answers, but I'm a good listener."

Judy invented a code for the more trying times. T.A.N.G. meant "Things Are Not Good," and when one of us said that, we knew the other one couldn't talk freely and we needed to pray.

Coni, our fifth friend with an Indian Summer birthday, had the talent of hair design. When she moved from a well-known Seattle salon to her home, Coni's Cottage for Hair became an oasis for anyone who came there. Coni offered her gift of hospitality, and pampered me with tea and cookies while I relaxed in an overstuffed chair. We found that we had much in common besides our birthdays. We prayed for our marriages and families, and each session with her seemed like therapy for our wounded hearts.

Our celebrations moved from the deli to a local restaurant that served to-die-for hot fudge sundaes. We all indulged for our birthdays. We had the luxury of living close for many years. Then I mustered the courage to move four and half hours away to join my husband after a year's separation.

The Birthday Club drove the winding road over the mountains to be with me in my new home that first year away. Being together eased my homesickness. The following year, I called each one with a special invitation.

"Of course we'll be there," they chorused. On a golden September morning (after our birthday celebration the night before), the Birthday

Club sat in the front row at our little log church when my husband and I renewed our wedding vows. We hardly had enough Kleenex to go around.

And every year since, we have found a place and time to meet to celebrate birthdays, friendship, and God's faithfulness, no matter how far we have to drive.

Deb Kalmbach is an author and speaker, and the co-author of *Because I Said Forever: Embracing Hope in a Not-So-Perfect Marriage.* She and her husband Randy live in Washington's beautiful Methow Valley with their dog, Kramer, and cat, Nip. Grown sons Chris and Jeremy live in the Seattle area.

Intimate Details:

I do not want to see you now and make only a passing visit; I hope to spend some time with you.

1 Corinthians 16:7

Inspirational Insight:

Getting together with friends can be one of the most important things you do for yourself. After taking care of everyone around you, gathering with close friends—letting your hair down and just enjoying each other—is a reward. But more than that, it's part of a healthy lifestyle.

Even Jesus knew the power of fellowship and friendship as He surrounded Himself with His disciples. He lived and traveled with people who shared His passion. In the same way, God doesn't expect us to muddle through life alone. He wants us to have friends who share our passions, celebrate our victories, and comfort us during difficulties.

If you're in need of friends who can be your sounding boards, cheerleaders, and prayer partners, ask God to help you develop those relationships. Then take the initiative and seek out friends who share your faith. Ask someone to lunch or coffee. Invite another mother to join you and your children for a play date. Talk to your neighbors. Don't think of the time you spend with them as frivolous. Instead, consider it inexpensive therapy that will keep you balanced during the hustle and bustle of life.

Heart to Heaven:

Lord, thank You for bringing godly friends into my life. I dedicate each one of them to You and recognize that they are gifts that I should value. You already know the commitments in my life, so please give me the wisdom to make time to invest in those friendships. Amen.

Chapter Two

FAVORITE FAMILY FRIENDS:

Extended Family Enriching Lives

I will not leave you comfortless: I will come to you.

John 14:18 KJV

As my children grab their backpacks and head out the door for school, I always say, "Let your light shine for Jesus. You may be the only Jesus some people ever see."

Abby and Allyson always smile and say, "We know, Mom." I'm sure they tire of hearing it. My hope is that they never tire of living it.

You may not wear a "Jesus Saves" T-shirt or post a "Got God?" bumper sticker on your SUV but you can still share the love of God. You can reach many hearts for Him simply by living out your faith on a day-to-day basis.

My friend Barb Morris is like that. She is soft-spoken—a very behind-the-scenes kind of Christian. She would never take credit for any good work, but her acts of kindness have not gone unnoticed by me. Ten years older than me, Barb used to help her mother babysit me while my parents played golf. I grew up thinking Barb was the coolest chick in the whole world. I wanted to be just like her.

I still do.

I want God's love to flow out of me as easily as it flows out of her. I want to do thoughtful things for others without expecting anything in return. I want to quietly impact lives for Christ—just like Barb has been doing her entire life. More than anything, I want the light of Jesus to shine so brightly in me that it warms those around me. I hope you'll share with me in that goal, and live the love every day. *MMA*

Heart to Heart:

Are you letting the love of God flow from you on a daily basis?

If not, why aren't you? Do you need a heart change? Are you afraid to reach out? Do you feel you have nothing to give? (Remember: God can mend your heart, fill you with faith and love, and help you to be more like Him.)

Moments with Mom Mom

Mary G. Johnson

As I stand at my sink snapping green beans, a batch my neighbor has given me from his kitchen garden, my mind wanders back to the first time I snapped beans, well over half a century ago.

My mind drifts back to my childhood and the special moments spent with my grandmother, Grace Fidler Hackney. To me, she was ancient, quiet, and calm. I liked to be with her. I had no idea this woman—weakened by time—was so strong. I had no idea that years later, I would still find strength and wisdom from those precious moments we shared together.

Bean Vines, Buzz Saws, and Banana Curls

I am eight, sitting alongside my grandmother in her front porch swing. We are shaded by bean vines that entwine strings she has stretched from her gingerbread porch roof down to stakes in her yard. We have picked enough of the long bumpy beans to fill a kettle. Now we sit with the kettle between us and stone crocks on our laps getting the beans ready to cook. I don't like doing this, but she has promised that if I help, she will pick roasting ears from her garden for supper. I like corn on the cob better than fudge.

Her crock is already half full of snapped beans. Mine holds perhaps two handfuls, and I had had trouble getting that many.

"You're not getting the strings off. Now watch again," she commands, pinching off an end and pulling the attendant green string down the length of the shaft, then pinching off the opposite end. Click, click, click. Bean pieces rain into her crock.

Her fingers are bent, but she breaks and strings beans as if she could do it forever—probably because she already has.

She is seventy-three. She has given birth to seven children. I am one of her nineteen grandchildren.

I am pigtailed and plain, a too-fat, too-freckled tomboy. I wear shorts, a halter top and no shoes. Even so, I have to push up my glasses because they keep sliding down my damp nose in this afternoon heat.

Mom Mom, as we grandkids call her, wears brown cotton pantyhose and lace-up oxfords. The front of her faded blue cotton housedress is covered by a washed-out green checked apron. I don't know exactly what undergarments she wears, but I do know there is a cotton slip under that dress. If the heat bothers her, she does not complain.

Her back is so humped that a third of her spine does not touch the slat-back swing. Wisps of white hair that have worked free from the soft bun atop her head, feather about her wrinkled, sunburned neck.

Despite the ruin that arthritis and osteoporosis have made of her bones, her gray eyes are clear and bright behind her steel-framed glasses.

She is wise. She knows the best things. She can turn a glass jar into a bank with a slot in the lid for pennies and nickels. She can make a buzz saw toy out of a string and a button. She fixes fried chicken on Sundays and sometimes makes homemade vanilla and lemon ice cream.

She has taught me and my cousins to play old games like I Spy and Capture the Flag and tag that involves a witch who is seeking her lost darning needle.

She knows which wild plants to gather to pound into a poultice to dry up poison ivy. Once when I had a really bad cough, she sewed me up in her homemade mustard plaster and saved me from having to get a penicillin shot.

When I ran a slew of splinters into my foot and limped around for two days screaming every time my mother tried to get near me with a needle, my grandmother came walking out of her pantry carrying a giant white bowl filled with hot water and Epsom Salts.

"Here. Put your foot in this," she directed.

After much complaining, I stuck the injured member down in the hot water.

Within twenty minutes, she handed me a needle.

"What am I supposed to do with this?" I asked.

"You try to get it out."

"Me? I can't do that."

"How do you know? You haven't even tried. You don't know what you can do 'til you try."

So I did. I quickly realized that I controlled the pain. If it hurt, I could stop. In a few minutes I had all those slivers out of my foot. I was exuberant and empowered because after that, I could remove my own splinters.

> Out of all that adversity and lack, the Good Lord raised a woman who relied on Him and who seemed to be able to deal with anything.
>
> —Mary G. Johnson

Mom Mom seemed to know how to help me feel better about myself. I longed for curly hair instead of my long, straight pigtails. One day when we were looking at old pictures, I saw a girl with long curls and said, "Wish my hair was like that."

The night before Easter, she washed my hair then sat me down in a kitchen chair. There was a pile of white cloth strips on the table.

"Is this gonna work?" I questioned.

"Never known it to fail," she answered.

She wound my damp hair around strips of cloth and tied the cloth to hold my hair until it dried. The next morning I sat in church alongside Mom Mom, but I didn't hear what the preacher said. I was too busy looking at the beautiful, long banana curls on my shoulders.

Learning from the School of Life

Today I wish I had listened more closely to this wise woman, especially when she spun out her memories of growing up in the 1800s.

She told of loving school, especially arithmetic, but not being allowed to attend school in the mornings when reading was taught because she had to stay home and do chores and cook the noon meal.

"Grace," the principal finally told her. "You do fine in the afternoons, but you need to come in the mornings so you can learn reading. You're holding back the class. Ask your folks if you can come in the mornings, too."

When she did, her mother said, "Well, you may as well quit. You're not learning anything anyway."

So, Grace Fidler's formal schooling ended when she was in the third grade. She became a fulltime housekeeper for her folks. She washed dishes standing on a wooden box. While still a child, she had to light her able-bodied mother's pipe with a broom straw and burning coal from the hearth while her mother sat and read.

Once when I asked Mom Mom about Christmas, she told about the gifts her sister and brothers were given.

"Laura got a handkerchief, John got a top, Will Hen (William Henry) got a ball, and Charlie got a marble. I think Jim got a new penny."

"What did you get, Mom Mom?" I asked.

She just shook her head as if it were not important.

"What'd you get for Christmas?" I demanded.

"There was nothing for me." she answered.

"NOTHING FOR CHRISTMAS! WHY, MOM MOM?"

She had nothing else to say.

As she became skilled in cleaning, laundry, cooking, canning, mending, sewing, and gardening, she worked for people in their homes. That's how she met and later married my grandfather, Riley Hackney. A mutual friend told Riley that if he cared for Grace Fidler, he should marry her and get her out of her parents' home as soon as possible. Soon after, Grace and Riley married and moved into their own home.

As a housewife and mother, Grace Fidler Hackney prepared three meals a day on a wood range, made her own lye soap, and scrubbed laundry for her husband and seven babies on a washboard, heating the water in a boiler atop a wood stove. She quilted with a stitch finer than any surgeon, made rag rugs on a loom nearly as large as her dining room and sold them to supplement the family income. She raised chickens. Fed and milked the family cow and churned butter. Made real mincemeat—eleven quarts at a time, mind you. Baked cream pies, rendered lard, and cooked apple butter in a copper pot in her side yard. Washed and laid out the dead and comforted the living. Buried her oldest son, who died with a ruptured appendix in 1910, and her oldest daughter, who succumbed to Spanish Flu in 1918. Went to church, taught Sunday school, and raised all her children and grandchildren to believe in Jesus.

She even taught us Bible verses in her home. Although she could barely read, she studied her Bible slowly, pointing her way through verses and chapters, books, and testaments with her index finger.

She not only knew the Word, she lived it.

Reared in a household where there was little human comfort, she must have learned early on that there was One who loved her. One whose heart must have broken when the little girl who loved to learn was not allowed to go to school, and when she was forced to assume work that her mother foisted off on her. Out of all that adversity and lack, the Good Lord raised a woman who relied on Him and who seemed to be able to deal with anything.

She went home to be with Him in 1959. But she comes to my mind often—especially when I feel weak and helpless and defeated. Her memory reminds me to turn my troubles over to Him because that's what Mom Mom did.

Someday I will go home, too, and get a great big hug from the One who loves us all. After that, if it's okay, I'd like to sit on His front porch and spend some time with Mom Mom.

Mary G. Johnson retired after a newspaper reporting career that spanned thirty-five years. She wrote for the *Bedford (Indiana) Times-Mail* for more than thirty years, winning Associated Press and Hoosier State Press Association awards. She makes her home in Orange County, Indiana.

Up Close and Personal:

Take a moment and list five people who have made a difference in your life. Maybe it's someone who took time for you when no one else would. Maybe it's your first-grade Sunday school teacher who taught you about Jesus. Maybe it's your favorite aunt who cared for you when no one else was there. Whoever they are, write their names and briefly describe how each one touched your life. Now, think for a minute, are you passing on the love that they showed to you? If so, record ways that you are living the love.

Green Ink

Laura L. Smith

The rush of Christmas was again upon me. I was opening a stack of Christmas cards, glancing quickly at photos of friends' children while listening to my four-year old daughter rehearse *The Little Drummer Boy* for her preschool Christmas program. My mind swirled with commitments, cookie recipes, and carols, and then it froze.

Staring at the letter in my hand, I couldn't draw oxygen from the air. My ears burned as if I had just come out of the December cold into a heated house.

In this envelope there was not a Christmas card. Instead, I held a letter signed by Helen's four children, letting me know of the unfortunate passing of their beloved mother. Forty-seven years had passed since Helen Tibbals walked into my mom's living room. I dropped to my kitchen floor; shaking while tears flowed down my face for the loss of this angel. And then, I smiled. Helen was in heaven where she had always belonged and from where she certainly had come.

A Technicolor Christmas

We heard the echo of someone knocking. Grandma Erskine opened the squeaky front door of her small home where my three brothers, my sister, my mother, and I lived. A slim, redheaded woman and her teenage boy stood smiling at us. I watched in awe as the two strangers carried armloads of packages wrapped in red with our names written on white tags in green ink. They also brought a pine tree, strings of colored lights, and glass ornaments, transforming the drab room from black and white to Technicolor. I backed against the threadbare couch to allow her and her son room to unload these treasures. They brought Christmas into our living room.

The woman in the green silk dress introduced herself as Helen Tibbals and her awkward-looking son as Todd Junior. She was a member of First Community Church, the same church we attended, and explained that she had taken a paper gift tag, shaped like the star of Bethlehem, off the Christmas tree standing in the church vestibule. It had our name on it.

She was all lipstick and smiles and smelled like the department store downtown. The sharp scent of peppermint filled my nose as she opened a box of candy canes and invited us to join in decorating the evergreen. All the while, she asked questions about us kids as if we were her own. I had so many questions for her, but was too shy to ask them. Where had this angel and her elf come from, and why did she care so much about my family?

Helen was the gift of Christmas present. A reminder that despite a father who had deserted us, a terminally-ill mother, and the fact that all five of us lived in a two-bedroom home with my mother and grandmother, God's hope and love still lived in the world.

My mom has told this tale so many times I can smell the scent of spruce and hear the clang of ornaments in the living room of their house on Hollywood Place.

Our Gift from God

Helen became much more than a Christmas gift; she became a part of our family. Until my mom and her siblings graduated from high school, Helen regularly brought them school supplies, new clothes, and chocolates. She even sent them to summer camp each year. When my grandmother struggled with breast cancer, Mom said Helen would bring candy bars and magazines to the small home as if she were Grandmother's sister. When my mom, aunt, and uncles were in college, Helen wrote them faithfully, always using her signature green pen. Helen attended my grandmother's funeral, my mother's graduation from high school, and my parents' wedding.

Helen's generosity expanded to the next generation as she adopted my brother and me as grandchildren, including us in her umbrella of selfless giving. She invited us to her home each summer for a feast and a stroll around her goldfish pond. Every birthday, gifts would arrive at our house, our names written across the top in green felt-tip marker.

I remember the excitement of seeing an envelope with my name scrawled in Helen's green ink every Easter and Valentine's Day. Poinsettias in December would bear her green signature and even the place cards at the annual Christmas dinner at her club, where she made sure the waiter kept our Shirley Temples refilled, were written in green ink.

When my husband, Brett, came home from work, he found me still weepy as I pulled a boiling pot of pasta off the stove, laid it in the sink, and scooped up our toddler, Matt, whose hands reached to the sky while saying, "Hold, Mama, hold!"

I pointed to where the tear-spotted letter lay limp on the counter.

Brett set his keys down and scanned the note. He turned and wrapped his strong arms around my quaking body. Soon I was able to exhale and push a smile onto my streaked face.

"Honey, can you get an extra name off the Giving Tree at church this year?" I swallowed hard, and then continued. "Helen came into my mom's life by picking her name from a tree. I would like to follow her example." A tear zigzagged down my cheek and then another.

"Of course," he smiled and kissed me on the tip of my nose.

The next day when Brett came home from work, he pulled two yellow pieces of paper cut in the shapes of mittens from the pocket of his parka.

"The directions said to put our name on the half of the tag still hanging on the tree, so the church would know who was responsible for that gift," Brett explained while easing his briefcase off his shoulder. "I guess that way, no child will go unaccounted for."

I nodded while drying my hands on the holly-embroidered towel by the kitchen sink.

"I wrote B. Smith on this tag, our tag," he said, holding up one of the canary-colored cards.

I started to walk toward him.

"And on this mitten," my husband's turquoise eyes twinkled, "I wrote H. Tibbals—in green ink."

Laura L. Smith's growing list of publications include: *Cantaloupe Trees*, a children's chapter book (Publish America 2001) and short stories that appear in *God Allows U-Turns* (Barbour Publishing 2001) and *God Allows U-Turns, A Woman's Journey* (Barbour Publishing 2002). She lives in Oxford, Ohio, with her husband and two children.

Open Arms, Open Heart

Leslie J. Wyatt

"Hey, she's my mom," my fiancé said. "Of course, she'll like you. She likes *me*."

"She likes you because you're her son," I answered, trying not to chew my fingernails. "She's never even met me."

"You'll be fine," he said with a smile. "Don't be nervous."

But I was nervous. Very nervous. Not many things in my life were comfortable on this day before our wedding rehearsal. My parents were not going to be involved in my wedding, friends were trying to fill in that cavernous gap, and I was about to meet my future mother-in-law for the first time.

She was flying in from sunny California, and I felt so dismally inadequate. Would she like me, or would she take one look and start trying to talk her son out of marrying me? All sorts of scenarios ran through my mind. I was a country mouse and she a smooth, cultured city mouse. My husband-to-be talked offhandedly of his mother's bridge parties, past Thanksgiving dinners with *real silver* silverware, and how their little dog, Pip, dug a hole in the wool carpet. Wool? I grew up in a house where the living-room "rug" was made of carpet samples of all heights, styles and colors.

He mentioned hating "cotillion" as if all the boys' mothers sent them to dance school, and casually dropped the fact that their grand piano used to belong to the famous singer Lily Pons. This future mother-in-law couldn't know how different my life had been. I'd grown up riding horses on the gravel roads of Montana, not skateboarding on the pavements of a California suburb. My siblings and I swam in the same pond the cows drank out of, not one of those aquamarine ovals that dotted my future husband's boyhood neighborhood.

She would be stylish. I was sure of it. Would I measure up? She had antiques from her mother's people in Scotland, and they used to vacation on Balboa Island. How would I find anything to talk about that wouldn't expose the great chasm between our two worlds?

The rental car pulled up in front of my fiancé's house. He kissed me for good luck and opened the door. There she was.

"David!" Her arms stretched out to hug her son. Then she turned to me. Would she extend polite fingers and avoid a direct gaze? Would she resent this girl whose family hadn't received her son?

Yet her arms were open. Tears were in her eyes. "And this must be Leslie," she said, and the warmth in those words wrapped my shrinking soul in comfort.

She folded me into a soft embrace and I smelled what would become a lovely fragrance to me—Chanel #5. Jane Wyatt was everything I had envisioned and more. Quiet culture oozed out of her without her even knowing it. For me, the evening transformed from an ordeal to a delight. In her brown eyes and open smile I found complete acceptance at a time when I so desperately needed it.

> She will never know what a gift she gave me when she came determined to love me. That simple, profound act touched me like nothing else could have done and enabled me to swing open the door of my heart and let her in.
>
> —Leslie J. Wyatt

In that season when my own parents were not available to me, this woman had flown to Montana determined to love the girl her son had decided to marry. She brought Dave's baby book and we looked over it together, she sharing little memories of his growing-up days, me drinking in details of a world so different from my own. Laughing at all my anecdotes, she hugged me often, and divided one of those huge chocolate bars "for a little dessert." It was the beginning: the beginning of a friendship that I treasure and one that has enriched my life in more ways than she could ever know. We have shared life together—the disappointments and triumphs, the fears and joys.

For years she made semiannual treks to Montana and then Missouri to visit, and has been the perfect grandmother to my children. Now she is eighty-three and travel is much harder for her, but we talk often, laughing about our shared passion for Oreo cookies (she likes the icing in the middle and I like the chocolate-cookie part) and how when she was a young mother, she and another young mom on her block locked themselves into a bathroom to inhale a pint of ice cream before their children discovered their absence and clamored for bites.

As I think back over the past twenty-plus years in which my mother-in-law and I have become fast friends, this one defining experience stands out from all others. She will never know what a gift she gave me when she came determined to love me. That simple, profound act touched me like nothing else could have done and enabled me to swing open the door of my heart and let her in.

Thank you, Jane. See you this summer, and this time *I'll* bring the Oreos.

Leslie J. Wyatt is a freelance writer for children and adults. She and her husband, Dave, have been blessed with six children, and live in Missouri on a "sort-of" farm with chickens, a garden, a dog, cats, and more than their fair share of mice.

A Real Woman

Sarah Crouch

"Happy Birthday to me! Happy Birthday to me! Happy Birthday, I'm fifty! Happy Birthday to me!"

She was never the conventional preacher's wife. Although she was the church organist (like so many women her age who married preacher boys), she preferred to make the pipes reverberate with a hearty rendition of "The Boogie-Woogie" than "Amazing Grace." So, it was not surprising that her attitude toward the big "5-0" birthday was unconventional, as well.

"Betty, you surprise me. I thought fifty-year-old women were supposed to have a little more dignity."

She was my spiritual mentor and musical partner at church (I was the church pianist), and I had always expected the best behavior from this genteel Southern lady.

"Well, not anymore!" she cackled. "I'm fifty now, and I've earned the right to say and do what I please!" Indeed, she was especially pleased with herself. She was still in good health, tall and attractive, with a few gray hairs peeking out from her stylish brown hairdo. She had a wicked sense of humor that often flashed at the most inopportune moments, usually in the middle of choir rehearsal.

A line from the hymn "Hiding in Thee" goes like this: "In the tempests of life, on its wide heaving sea." When we sang this phrase in rehearsal, Betty took that moment to gag as if literally heaving up her supper, leaving the rest of us unable to ever sing that hymn again without snickering.

At after-church fellowships, she accompanied her husband on the piano as he sang beautiful love songs. At least, he tried to sing them. This stately, dignified pastor stood looking bemused as Betty's fingers ran up and down the keys playing long and lavish introductions. As he inhaled to sing, she would add another few measures to confuse and frustrate him. After two or three unsuccessful attempts to begin, she finally allowed him his big moment. It was all part of the act—the patient and calm husband and his talented, but unaware wife—and we loved it. So, how could she possibly be any less concerned with what people thought of her than she already was?

> *She realized, at the ripe age of fifty, that it was more important to be a real woman than to be a perfect woman.*
>
> —Sarah Crouch

"I don't understand, Betty. Haven't you been doing what you wanted to do all these years?" I asked.

"Not really," she replied. "I've taught Sunday School, played the organ, and given my kids the evil-eye when they were disturbing the peace during church services. I've attended ladies' mission meetings and enough covered-dish suppers to last a lifetime. I've always been where I was expected to be. Now it's time for myself. Now it's time to do things for me."

And what did she want to do? She wanted to go to the opera instead of another committee meeting. She wanted to start a class for single adults instead of teaching the deacons' wives. She wanted to wear jeans and denim shirts. She wanted to be herself.

I watched this wonderful woman who loved God with all her heart take a courageous step. In 1976, when she turned fifty, it was not common for a preacher's wife to be so assertive. These gracious and talented women were supporters behind the scenes, and accepted the unwritten rules of congregational behavior that were already in place. But Betty embraced these traditions and transformed them with her own unique style.

She continued to serve her church and support her husband in his ministry, but she did it on her own terms. On the surface, she laughed at herself and her rebelliousness, but deep in her heart she maintained an enduring love for the people of her church and community. She realized, at the ripe age of fifty, that it was more important to be a real woman than to be a perfect woman. She knew that she needed to be true to herself, to love the woman God had created her to be, with all her zany antics and shocking commentary of church happenings.

That's what she taught me, a twenty-six-year-old people-pleaser. She taught me to let go of others' expectations and to find my worth in God's acceptance and mercy. She taught me to laugh at my mistakes and to find joy in unexpected places. She showed me that true friendship is never about age, but about the connection of two kindred souls.

When my father died, she brought me to her house for the day. I thought I was there to consult with her about funeral music, but I was really there to experience the soothing presence of a safe haven. It was there that I expressed my personal grief—away from family members who needed me to be strong. A more conventional friend might have tried to pat me on the arm and say, "There, there, you'll be okay." But she knew I wouldn't be okay for a long time, and her silent acceptance allowed me to scream and yell my hurt to God.

Years later, when her husband died, I was in her home offering my own words of comfort. "Don't you cry!" she admonished me. Instead, we laughed and shared funny memories about the man my daughters loved as a surrogate grandfather. It comforted me to learn that the music she and I played together in church and recorded, had brought him peace during his final days.

So, when I turned fifty, guess whose advice I followed?

"I'm going to do and say what I please, because I've earned the right."

My family wasn't surprised to hear those words from me. Betty, my friend, my mentor, my spiritual mother, had taught me well. I was ready to be the real woman God had made me to be, and I've been racing to catch up. I learned from Betty that doing and saying what I want isn't about stepping on feelings or being selfish, it's about allowing God to transform a shy, people-pleasing church pianist into a woman who isn't afraid to open her heart and be vulnerable. It's about having the courage to set aside others' expectations and focus on pleasing God. It's about stepping out in faith and loving the woman God loves. Thank you, Betty.

Sarah Crouch is a freelance writer and a piano teacher in Cedar Hill, Texas. She lives with her husband, two daughters, and a really cute dog.

Originally appeared in Simple Pleasures Of Friendship published by Conari Press, imprint of Red Wheel/Weiser, York Beach, ME.

Celebrate the Moment:

This week, do something special to carry on the love that you've been shown by that favorite family friend. Maybe you can take a less fortunate child shopping for school clothes. Maybe you can offer to watch that frazzled new mother's children one afternoon. Or, maybe you can just send a card to thank someone for her kindness. (If you do, go ahead and use green ink!)

Intimate Details:

Love is patient, love is kind. It does not envy, it does not boast, it is not proud. It is not rude, it is not self-seeking, it is not easily angered, it keeps no record of wrongs. Love does not delight in evil but rejoices with the truth. It always protects, always trusts, always hopes, always perseveres. Love never fails.

1 Corinthians 13:4–8

Inspirational Insight:

Just as a pebble tossed into the middle of a lake causes many ripples, so do people in that big lake we call "life." We just never know how many ripples we make or how many people we touch over the course of our lives.

As you take time to reflect on those special friends or extended family members who have impacted you through their timeless advice, colossal kindness, or limitless love—consider this: You, too, are impacting others right now. You may be unaware, but you are touching many lives through your daily actions and words. That should both excite you and challenge you.

I'm sure Helen Tibbals, with her green ink pen, never had any idea how many hearts she touched with the love of God. But her legacy of love continues even today.

Heart to Heaven:

Lord, thank You for placing special people in my life. I know that You have used these friends as an extension of Your love to me. Help me, Lord, to be ever mindful that I am touching others' lives—either good or bad—every day. Help me to let Your light shine in me and through me so that I, too, can be an extension of Your love to those around me and beyond. I love You, God. Amen.

Chapter Three

ACROSS THE MILES:

Distance Can't Weaken Friendship

How blessed all those in whom you live, whose lives become roads you travel.

Psalm 84:5 MSG

"Absence makes the heart grow fonder," Thomas Haynes Bayly wrote. I happen to agree.

Long-distance friendships are familiar to me.

During my four years at college, I met friends from every corner of the United States plus several from Australia, Africa, Europe, and various Caribbean Islands. After college, we dispersed, returning to our little corners or forging ahead to new places.

As I reflect on my long-distance friendships, one in particular comes to mind: Lynda. We met during my senior year. My then boyfriend/today husband had known Lynda for years, considering her one of his closest friends. After college, Lynda and I solidified our friendship when we lived in the same area. Both of us have a penchant for experimental cooking, Jane Austen movies, and literature. For two years, we joyfully dragged each other to art exhibits and tea rooms until Lynda's desire for adventure took her to teach kindergarteners in Indonesia. Today, though back in the States, she still lives far away.

She is still a dear friend.

Now separated by the miles, we continue to rejoice in each other's lives. I was ecstatic when, after holding out for Mr. Right, she called to say she had found him. In turn, she consoled me when I shared my dilemmas about a career change. And we still keep each other up-to-date on the latest artsy movies.

We've discovered that close friends aren't easy to find. They're not the ones with whom you only share your victories. They're also the ones with whom you share your disappointments and fears. When you've discovered someone who can share both sides of the spectrum—regardless of how close or far away they live—you aren't willing to let that go. You realize it's just too precious. *GM*

Heart to Heart:

Do you have close long-distance friendships?

Have they been successful or have they drifted away?

What does it require to keep distant friendships strong?

A Shared Moment

Diane H. Pitts

Promptly at two o'clock, I heard the car door slam and conjured up the smell of scones and tea biscuits even before the back door opened.

Lisa had brought afternoon tea!

She greeted me with a booming laugh and a basket brimming with a visual feast. Starched linen napkins, an English teapot and cozy, Battenberg lace runner, and Delft blue cups met my gaze. My nose caught the whiff of freshly baked goodies hidden from sight; what tea would accompany them today? Earl Grey or English breakfast? Maybe I would splurge with something bolder like an Indian or Kenyan tea.

Soon the empty table was transformed, creating a haven for two friends to share a moment in time. The lace runner alighted on the table like a butterfly seeking rest. Fingering the napkins, I relaxed with the knowledge of what was to come.

Enjoying the ritual we loved so well, Lisa and I traded initial pleasantries as the retreat proceeded. I placed the teapot and cups in their accustomed positions while Lisa apportioned the delicacies on china plates. Within minutes, the interchange drifted toward the second level of conversation—concerns and reports of family matters.

An unseen butler must have continued the hosting duties because we lost ourselves in the tea-time experience. Sipping and tasting, we plunged into the sea of thought-provoking conversation, coming up only for the air of tangents. Any topic or wistful yearning surfaced at will. Lisa and I floated along in the current of the moment and examined ideas like treasures from the ocean floor. The tide's ebb and flow eventually deposited us on the sand of scone crumbs, in the shadow of a tea cozy.

Reluctantly, we folded our napkins and repacked the familiar basket as the clock chimed three times. Another tea time closed, and yet this one was unlike all the others because it held an air of finality; Lisa was moving across the ocean to Africa where her family would work as missionaries in an orphanage. We hesitated to voice our thoughts.

Finally, we simultaneously clutched the basket as each one reached for an errant corner of the lace runner. Laughter broke the seriousness that had descended like a drizzling rain. Wordlessly, our eyes and hearts said, "Until next time," for the simplicity of shared moments forges a friendship that spans distance as well as time.

Wordlessly, our eyes and hearts said, Until next time, for the simplicity of shared moments forges a friendship that spans distance as well as time.

—Diane H. Pitts

Unhurriedly, she gathered the items and turned to leave. I watched and listened as the front door opened and closed. I looked back toward the table and noticed Lisa had forgotten her tea bags. I started to knock on the kitchen window to get her attention, but then I realized the bags were not really forgotten. Instead, she had left a reminder of a simple pleasure of friendship—a shared moment.

Today we communicate primarily by e-mail and yet the friendship has only strengthened. Although we live on different sides of the globe, the miles have only served to make us reach deeper for words to describe what God is doing in our lives. Recently, a certain joy has begun to seep out every time I smell tea or look at my china, for this fall, tea time will live again! Lisa comes home on furlough!

I can see it now. The car door will slam, and the laughter will bubble out. We will pick up where we left off, yet each will bring far more tangents to the conversation. A friendship born of the Spirit defies distance by growing richer with time and only increasing in fragrance.

Diane H. Pitts resides on the Gulf Coast with her husband and three boys. She works as a physical therapist and writes about faith in the home, as well as the medical arena. She enjoys other roles of educator, missions advocate, musician, and best of all, friend.

Up Close and Personal:

Describe a friend who lives far away. How has distance affected your friendship? Why has it remained strong, or what has caused it to weaken?

Westward Bound

Lisa Dahlstrom

I had dreaded this moment for weeks, but time had sped by impervious to my emotions. And now we had to say goodbye.

Around us were attentive waiters, the enticing aroma of grilled steak, and a rich décor. Normally, this would be a wonderful treat. I was in a nice restaurant with my best friend and had seriously slipped my stay-at-home mom leash. Can anyone say "party"?

But instead it was a somber meal. She tried to imagine what the future might hold in the small mountain town 1,800 miles away where she knew no one except her sister. And yet, she knew well the quiet Voice leading her there.

She trusted Him.

I tried *not* to imagine the upcoming days and weeks without dropping in to see her on an impulse, not having our daily phone conversations, and not feeling her hand on top of mine as she prayed for my marriage, my children—all of the deep concerns of my heart.

I would have to trust Him.

Desperately I wanted at this moment of parting to say something of value. Something that would stand through time. Something to try and express the depth of my feelings for her. It might be the last time we ever saw each other. She was no longer young, and her health was not the best.

Trying as hard as I could to be positive, I took a deep breath and began.

"In many of the stories we read," I tentatively started, referring to the simple pioneer stories we loved, "the friend who stays behind gives something dear to the friend forging ahead as a symbol of their relationship."

I worried that it sounded hokey, but she didn't laugh. She nodded her head showing she understood. I handed her the small box, embracing her with my eyes.

When she saw the marquis-cut blue topaz ring, tears ran down her cheeks. It had always been my favorite ring, and she knew it. Carefully, my mother slipped the ring over the white line where my father's ring had rested for more than fifty years—it looked so right.

It was right.

She would wear a visible reminder of my love, this pioneer. And I would have the pleasure of knowing that my ring adorned the hand that had carried me, stroked away my nightmares as a child, helped pack my belongings each time I moved, and given my firstborn child a bath when I didn't know how—my mother, my best friend.

When I look down at my ringless finger these days, I am reminded of my mother's love. Like a ring, it can never be broken. Miles may separate us, but her love is forever with me.

Lisa Dahlstrom lives in Fort Worth, Texas, with her husband, two young children, and cat, "Jazzie." When not homeschooling, she quilts, reads, writes, and enjoys imbibing tea.

Her Name Is Love

Anne Worth

I met Dr. Patricia Love twenty years ago when we were still in graduate school, and yes, Love is her real name. She and I were among the few women in the department, so we spent a lot of girl time together until I married and moved to Dallas. Even though we did not see each other as frequently after that, I knew we would be special friends for life.

Ten years later, I was divorced and living alone when the doctor diagnosed a problem in my uterus and told me that I must have a hysterectomy. I was not a Christian at the time, and I had a rather limited support circle.

Okay, I can handle this, I thought. So, I looked at my work schedule and made the necessary arrangements.

Coincidentally, Pat, who then lived four hours away, called to say hello the week before my surgery. When I told her my plans, she asked who was going to be with me during the surgery. I told her a friend would drop me off at the hospital and then my aunt was coming two days later when I went home.

"I mean, who will be there when you wake up?" she asked more specifically.

"No one," I replied. "I will be sedated, and I won't even know if anyone is there or not. The nurses will take care of me." So proud of my self-sufficiency, it did not even occur to me to ask someone to sit in the waiting room while I was in surgery or to be in the room to help me after it was over.

"This will not do!" she said. "When you come back to your room, you need to see someone's smiling face who loves you. Heck, you need someone to get things for you when you get back to the room. You can't be calling the nurses to do little things a friend can do. And it would be nice to have someone praying for you. Now, who can do that for you?"

"Pat, I don't need anyone to be there. I am going to be all right," I protested.

"No, this won't do!" she exclaimed again. "I am going to come up there and be with you."

"With your schedule? How can you get away?"

"I will."

"Pat, this is just not necessary."

"I don't want to hear another word from you unless it is to tell me that there is someone else that you would rather have with you."

Feeling quite touched by my friend's generosity, I weakly said, "Well, I am just overwhelmed by your concern, and I simply don't know what to say."

"Good, don't say anything. I hope you are overwhelmed by love! You are my sister, Anne. Now we need to get down to details. When do you go to the hospital, and what do you have to do the day before? When is your aunt coming? Who is picking her up at the airport? Will you already have groceries in the house?"

She went on asking questions as though she had an imaginary checklist of pre- and post-surgical details that needed her attention. Once she had all the necessary information, she informed me that she would arrive early enough to take me to the pre-op appointments at the hospital on the day before the surgery.

She drove me to the hospital that morning, and she sat on my bed while I waited to go in for blood tests and an EKG. She held my hand as we talked about the difficult things one should discuss before rolling into surgery. We laughed and cried at the same time. I don't think I had ever felt so close to a woman before. I had never been close to my mother and I didn't have a real sister, but I knew this is how a close family would feel. Grateful for her generosity, both of time and spirit, she was the Savior's loving Spirit that day and in the days that followed.

It was wonderfully reassuring to see her face in the recovery room and to know she waited for me outside. And when I had a severe reaction to the morphine, I was fortunate to have her there to help with the extra care I needed.

Today, I am blessed to be a Christian and I have many sisters I can count on, but as long as I live, I will never forget what Pat did for me. Her actions made a lonely woman feel loved. Actions do speak louder than words.

Thank you, Pat Love. Your name fits you beautifully!

Anne Worth has been a counselor for twenty-five years. She loves to tell others how Jesus has redeemed her life. She is active in the prayer ministry of her church and in several Christian groups including the "Fellowship Go Girls" in Dallas, Texas.

Solace from Sign Language

Elizabeth Hanniel

I had no idea when I was searching for a sign-language teacher for my homeschooled son, I would find a lifelong friend.

"Well, you have come to the right person," Elaine spoke confidently over the phone after I explained my need. "Not only am I a sign-language instructor, but I have been praying for another student."

"You have been praying for a student? We have been praying for help," I shared.

"Where do you live? Anywhere near me?" Elaine questioned without delay.

"On the west side of town, within a few miles of your address," I answered. Unbelievably close, I thought.

"How about I come to your home once a week? This would be in addition to the sign-language classes where he would meet some great students his age. I think this is my answer to prayer!" she exclaimed.

Although I am normally quite reserved with my emotions, I began to cry with relief. Thank You, God!

When Tragedy Strikes

The year progressed with my son Jeffery learning to order food and give directions in sign language. Elaine worked diligently to involve my son in her group, warming us to her even more. Over the summer, she held a camp in her studio where her students learned to sign "Sitting on the Dock of the Bay" and other summer-themed concepts.

Jeffery continued learning, and I continued thanking God for Elaine.

The next Thanksgiving, Elaine stayed in town, while the rest of her relatives needed to be in various other places. Unperturbed at being alone, she used the time wisely, working on her writing assignments. We e-mailed back and forth, as I cajoled her to join us for Thanksgiving dinner.

"Thank you for the invitation," she wrote, "but I intend to wear pink fuzzy slippers and my terry-cloth bathrobe, pounding out these stories, which are due."

Knowing she had stayed home, I e-mailed her over the Thanksgiving holidays when my husband, Chris, was suddenly hospitalized with a rare disease. I urgently asked her to pray with me, and then days later, I shared the unthinkable news—Chris had died. So many of our friends and family were out of town, but Elaine never left. It was such a gift. She arrived with warm homemade cherry cobbler in a flowered cloth-covered dish. The offering was a popular dessert among the visitors, and gave a nice aroma to the dining area.

In planning the memorial service, I asked Elaine to perform sign language as the vocalist sang "On Eagle's Wings." It was tender and breathtaking: The silent signs danced with the deep voice. For my son and his friends, her familiar face and role cast a reassuring balm in the sanctuary.

Bridging the Distance

Since we had known Elaine, we had always prayed for each other. For many months, she had asked us to pray that her house in another state would sell. Buyer after buyer fell through, and even my son was discouraged for her. Ultimately, with a home unsold and her husband's job loss, she decided to move out of state.

Life without Mrs. Elaine as our tutor? It couldn't happen. Jeffrey found a fantastic solution: Internet classes. Elaine went right to work on the arrangements, and she has continued as his tutor despite the miles of separation. Often she ends her grading of his writing assignments with "I Love You."

For Christmas, she mailed him a rare book for his collection of *Tom Swift, Jr.* series. "I love her," Jeffrey said simply as he held the rough binding on the treasured book. By preventing my son from suffering another loss so soon after his father's passing, she endears herself to me over and over.

"I love her, too," I contributed, and in her absence, we gave each other a bear hug.

Our friendship has not only survived the move, but actually thrived. In my saddest moments, often around midnight, I will expose my fears and grief to my Internet buddy. Never has she failed to greet me in the morning with an e-mail exhortation. "Elizabeth, I know you are missing Chris, but hold on! Stay focused on this world. Don't wish to join him on the other side—don't go there!" Elaine barked. "Work in the garden, digging around in the soil of life. Make plans with your son. Pray for comrades in your grief. Stay here in thought and body!"

Her words cut through the electronic wires with the direct admonishment I sorely needed to hear in my depression. Many of my local friends thought I was so strong, but Elaine knew differently.

Recently it was her turn to write the unthinkable: Her son-in-law had died in a traffic accident. From afar, I offered hope and experience as a young widow, and prayed unceasingly for her to retain good health, despite her loss of sleep.

With Elaine's photo posted on my refrigerator, I daily send warm hugs and the sign language gesture for love. Although I miss our regular visits around my kitchen table, I marvel at our closeness, which started as a search for a sign-language instructor, and continues to provide solace for whatever search our life journey brings.

Elizabeth Hanniel lives in Texas with her son and mixed-breed dog, Jada. She is ever so grateful for the friendships of women who have comforted and listened to her struggles surrounding the death of her husband, as well as the decision to homeschool.

Celebrate the Moment:

Make a point to connect with a distant friend through a letter, card, or e-mail, especially if you haven't seen or heard from her in a long time.

Old Friends

Karen Nordberg Sanders

Fine friendships made while we are young
Hold fast though lives become far-flung.
We keep in touch by note and card,
Through joy-filled years and trials hard,
To meet again when hairs turn gray.
'Tis like we'd never been away.
Our love and laughter of the past
Lives on. True friendships always last!

Karen Nordberg Sanders is a veteran educator, active Lutheran, and freelance writer from Richardson, Texas. She enjoys old friends from three alma maters: Hood College (BA, English), Texas Woman's University (M.Ed.), and University of North Texas (Ph.D.). Karen is the mother of three and grandmother of nine.

Intimate Details:

Dear friend, I pray that you may enjoy good health and that all may go well with you, even as your soul is getting along well. It gave me great joy to have some brothers come and tell about your faithfulness to the truth and how you continue to walk in the truth.

3 John 2–3

Inspirational Insight:

"Don't be afraid of the goodbyes," my stepmother, Patty, once told me. She warned me not to close myself off from people just because I'd one day leave them behind. She was right.

We live in a mobile world where the days of growing up and settling down in the same area are gone. Of course, there are still those who do that, but there is a large percentage that moves around due to job changes or a desire to see the world. As you journey through life, you'll inevitably leave behind friends or be left behind.

Don't let "out of sight, out of mind" be your signature. Do yourself a favor and hold onto your friendships. If you have a friend who moves, fire up the telephone and e-mail lines. Your friendship will mean the world to her in the midst of change. And, if you're the one who moves, reach out to your friends. Don't close yourself off and believe that you have to go it alone. Even though they aren't with you physically, your friends can still help you stay sane in the midst of transition.

And after the move is over, a long-distance friend can always give you the objectivity and perspective you need in your life. She's far enough away from the situations and people surrounding you that she can give you valuable feedback. Then, you can do the same for her. The advice, encouragement, and prayers you'll share with each other will be powerful—

maybe even more powerful than when you were together. Distance will never weaken the cords of friendship, because miles can't separate hearts.

Heart to Heaven:

Lord, thank You for allowing me to be the kind of friend who can keep a friendship strong even when I'm far away. Help me to not be "out of sight, out of mind" with my friends, but teach me to be a faithful companion. Amen.

Chapter Four

SISTER TO SISTER:

Sisters by Blood, Friends by Choice

May the Lord make your love increase and overflow for each other.

1 Thessalonians 3:12

"Stop it, Ally!" screamed her older sister, Abby.

Still, the taunting continued in the backseat.

"Abby is a stupid head!" Ally shouted in a sing-songy manner.

"That's enough," I interjected, glaring at my two preschoolers in the rearview mirror.

After a few moments of quiet bliss, Abby leaned forward and very seriously asked, "Mommy, can we just sell Ally?"

"No, I think we'd better keep her," I answered, trying to stifle my giggles.

Out of that encounter with my bickering babes, my book *Sister for Sale* was birthed—a picture book released in March 2002 by Zonderkidz. And it's been quite popular. You know why? Because big sisters and little sisters all over the world can relate to the book's title—*Sister for Sale*.

I'll admit, as much as I adore my big sister, Martie, there have been times I would've slapped a price tag on her forehead and put her in our annual yard sale. Martie, being the older sister, left some pretty perfect footsteps to follow in, and I soon discovered that I didn't like following in anyone's footsteps.

Still, without Martie in my life, I don't know where I'd be. She's quick to come to my defense if anyone "messes with her little sister." Yet, she's the first to let me know when I'm out of line. You might say—she keeps me balanced. We've shared many joyous occasions together—our weddings, our babies, our career triumphs. And we've been there for each other through all of life's storms—the demise of her first marriage, my troubled pregnancies, our father's death. We are very close—despite the seventeen-year age difference.

I once gave her a plaque that said, "Sisters by blood, friends by choice." That's really how I feel about her. She's not just my sister—she's my friend. I only hope that my little girls will someday enjoy each other as much as Martie and I do. Until then, I'll don my black-and-white shirt and keep my whistle handy. *MMA*

Sisters

Cathy Coraccio

When I see you—
The babies that I made,
You play, laugh, you dance together—
As if this is how it has always been,
As if I had nothing to do with it.
And I guess you were made for each other
In some plan that threw my life around
In order to give you one another—
So you can walk hand in hand,
As Sisters.

Cathy Coraccio lives in Brooklyn, Connecticut, with her husband, Philip, and her three girls: Summer, Mary, and Megan. She has two stepchildren: Anthony and Contessa. She is currently raising her children while pursuing her writing career.

Heart to Heart:

If you're sisterless, have you ever longed for a sister? Why? What treasures would a sister bring into your life? Do you have a friend or a relative who serves as a substitute sister in your life?

If you have a sister, have you ever longed to be an only child? (Be honest.) If so, did you have those feelings because of jealousy? How do you feel about your sister today—this very moment?

A Perfectly Timed Answer

Julie Durr

In the dirt next to our driveway, I traced circles with a stick. The day was warm. I felt terribly alone. My brothers had gone to play baseball in the field with the neighbors. There were boys everywhere, but I didn't have anyone to play with and being bored wasn't an option. So I traced circles in the sand alone.

For a long time I sat there before I decided I would take a memory moment. My Dad had said that if I wanted to remember something, I should just tell myself to remember it. I started, "I will remember this." I visualized the surroundings and made a sensory picture. I picked up a handful of sand and let it sift through my fingers. I wondered, *How long must I feel this way?*

I looked to the heavens, tired of feeling alone, and asked God for a sister. I wondered if He would answer. I wondered if He had heard me. Somewhere within me, I knew the answer. He had heard me, and my request for a sister had been denied.

The years passed, and occasionally I would remember my request. My memory moment would flash in my mind, and I would push it away. I already had the answer.

I graduated from high school and went to Michigan Technological University. During that time, I found out that my dad had cancer and was dying. Again, I felt alone. I longed for a sister to share with, to cry with, to understand me. God sent me a friend but not a sister.

My mom called me at college to let me know when my dad had passed away. For years after, every time the telephone rang, I wondered if it would bring more bad news.

Several years later, my mom remarried. I thought, *Maybe now I will get a sister.* The stepfamily included two brothers, but no sisters. The children from both families were all adults and going their own ways. This created a division of Mom's kids and Gerry's. We didn't have a cohesiveness of a past together. It was a tough adjustment to consider each other family. We tried. I speculated, *If only one of them had been a sister, it might be easier.*

At the age of twenty-seven, I married. For Christmas, my husband and I traveled back to see my family. My mom had hung stockings with my name and my husband's name on a shelf. Trying to inspire us, she hung a tiny stocking in between ours. *Hint, hint.* We talked about how we were trying to have a baby, but it hadn't happened yet. Noticing that my mom had gained some weight and had been sick a lot lately, I kidded her, "Why don't you have a baby? You're still newlyweds. Are you sure you're not pregnant?"

> I looked to the heavens, tired of feeling alone, and asked God for a sister. I wondered if He would answer. I wondered if He had heard me.
>
> —Julie Durr

"*No, no!*" Mom explained, "I'm almost fifty, and I've already entered the change. It's just the flu."

"I'm just kidding, Mom," I teased, "but you know I always wanted a sister. I even prayed about it once. You should see a doctor if you don't get better soon."

About a month later, the phone rang.

Please, not more bad news, I thought.

I answered the phone. It was my mom.

"Maybe you should sit down," she started.

I sank into a chair, physically and emotionally.

"I went to the doctor," she continued. "He found something during the exam."

Oh no. Please not cancer, I thought.

"He thought it might be a tumor or a cyst and sent me to get a sonogram," she said.

"And?!" I nervously prompted.

"They didn't find a cyst," she added. "Are you sitting down?"

"Yes," I answered, prepared for the worst.

"They found a baby girl," she shared. "You're finally going to have a sister. I'm about four months pregnant!"

Twenty years after I had prayed for a sister, Anna was born. Anna is now thirteen, and she has been the sister I always wanted. We share a love of books, chocolate, horses, and God. I love watching as Anna plays with my children. She is like a big sister to them. Anna has also become a connection between two grown stepfamilies. She is a living bond between us. God answered my prayer.

His answer was more than I expected. He gave me a surprise, an answer, a sister, a bond between two families, and a big sister for my own children. Her birth was a miracle perfectly timed and a prayer completely answered.

Julie Durr, a mother, a homeschooler, a wife, and a writer began her career as a freelance writer in January 2001. Julie has been published online at *Senior Citizens Magazine* and *Wee Ones Magazine*. Recently, she completed a vocational biography. She combines her love of writing with her priorities, the three "F's": (F)aith, (F)amily, and (F)riends.

Up Close and Personal:

Think about your sister. What makes her so special and unique? Now, list the qualities in her that you most admire. Do you share those same qualities? Write some of the personality traits that make you special, too. (This is not the time to be modest—be honest.) Are they the same?

What's Special?

Mishel Hawas

What's so special about you?

Is it the way you forgave me
when I told Mom you cut
all the hair off the dog,
even though it was me?

Is it the way you forgave me
for sticking a candy up my nose
and then putting it back in the bowl
so you couldn't enjoy them?

Is it the way you forgave me
for running into your room
shouting "You're too bony!"
over and over again?

Is it the way you forgave me
for not calling you for years,
for thinking I could find a better friend
in this world than you?

Or is it the way you don't have to forgive me
for any of these things,
because you know me well enough to know
that I don't always do the right things?

Or is it the way you don't have to forgive me
because you love me enough
to love me for who I am,
even all the bad things that I am?
Or is it the way that you know
I love you, too,
even if I've not yet
been able to say it?

I think it's all of these things
and a million more things
that make you so special
to me.

Mishel Hawas is a writer, poet, and essayist based in Australia. She lives in a small country town with her husband and spends her days writing articles, stories, essays, poems, and opinion pieces. Her work has been published in various anthologies, magazines, and e-zines in Australia, America, and Great Britain.

Twins and Friends

Patti Iverson

Peggy is more than a sister. She's my twin! We are separate bodies, different personalities, disparate lives, but one heart and one Savior. She lives in California, and I call her the "wicked (say with a growl) twin of the south," while I, in Oregon, am the "good (falsetto voice) twin of the north." Nobody buys it, but it always gets a laugh.

Memories are tricky details of life. We shared the same experiences growing up, but for some reason, Peggy's memories diverge from mine. Of course, I say, "Peggy, you just remember wrong." That always goes over real well.

Los Angeles in the 1950s was a golden era. Orange trees, Hollywood movie stars, clean air, and good people were the norm. At the wee age of five, we traipsed all over our small town of South Pasadena visiting (harassing?) neighbors, and going to the corner grocery store. We each guarded the quarter in our sweaty palms to buy a pack of Pall Mall cigarettes for Mom and a half-gallon of milk for Daddy.

The big kids on the block put on shows with music, drama, and magic acts. At twilight, everybody joined up for Hide and Seek. I recall being mad because Peggy wanted to hide alone, without me. How dare she assert her autonomous nature so early in life!

We shared many fun times—playing house, dress up, arts and crafts, swimming, and all the other childhood joys during that delightful decade. We also fought our sibling battles with fervor worthy of the Civil War. Like those soldiers, we always had times of socializing and sharing common bonds between the bloodshed. Once, I tied Peggy up during a rousing round of Cowboys and Indians and pushed her off the front porch. Oh, how I cried along with her as if it were *my* tooth that was chipped and bloodied. She got me back, though. It sure wasn't nice when she zoomed me down the lengthy banister during a sisterly skirmish!

Occasionally, we came together to join forces against a common enemy. One Easter Sunday, as we proudly walked up Meridian Avenue in our holiday finery with our new plush bunnies under our arms, a nasty boy named Ricky started his usual bullying. Well, ya just don't mess with the twins on a religious holiday! We started fighting like a couple of bantam hens. Flying bonnets, ripped lacy white socks, and frilly dresses didn't matter. Maryjanes, muddied and scuffed, kicked poor Ricky in his backside. No more problems ever ensued with that neighborhood bully!

Our parents died when we were still in school, which strengthened the twinship bond even more. Years have flown by. Marriages, babies, and life challenges have brought us closer as twins and friends.

—Patti Iverson

The Twinship Bond

Our parents died when we were still in school, which strengthened the twinship bond even more. Years have flown by. Marriages, babies, and life challenges have brought us closer as twins and friends. We really do think alike.

ESP is an actual thing between twins. We have held the same jobs although thousands of miles apart—clowns, preschool teachers, telephone operators, and activity directors. One year we mailed each other the exact same tote bag for our birthday. I thought she was just being cheap and had sent it back to me!

Now as middle-aged matrons, we continue to live, learn, and love as twins with the best bond of all, joyfully being part of the Yahweh Sisterhood with unconditional love for each other. (Even if she still has a faulty memory!)

Patti Iverson lives in Medford, Oregon, with her fire chief husband. She is a writer, part-time clown and Mrs. Santa Claus, and to be more spiritual, she also leads a Bible study. She does calligraphy and cooks while keeping in touch with her two grown children. She's been blessed by many glorious women in her life.

Celebrate the Moment:

Do something nice for your sister this week. C'mon, you know you want to! Since there isn't a national holiday called, "Sisters Day," why not start one? Choose a day and make special plans (maybe even a weekend trip) with your sister.

Particular Joy

Mindy Starns Clark

Indian-style
you both sit, knees touching, on a worn blue blanket in the middle of the yard.
The first nice day of Spring and you wanted a picnic, so you share apple slices tipped with peanut butter, a jug of water, two orange plastic cups with lids.

You talk softly. And for the blessed space of an hour, maybe more,
there is no fussing, no fighting, no pulling hair,
only giggles and whispers and sticky peanut-butter fingers.
At three and five you can't see what you have, but it's there.

On this first nice day of Spring when I pause from my garden digging
and watch you
and relish
the blond curls that encircle you like halos
the tiny bodies outlined by sunlight
the smell of earth and apples and little girls.
I wonder at the particular joy of having a sister, a secret I never knew,
and my prayer is that you will always, always
treasure each other as much as you do
right now.

Mindy Starns Clark is the author of the Million Dollar Mysteries series from Harvest House Publishers, including *A Penny for Your Thoughts, Don't Take Any Wooden Nickels,* and *A Dime a Dozen.* Originally from Louisiana, she lives with her husband and two daughters near Valley Forge, Pennsylvania.

Intimate Details:

Treat...older women as mothers, and younger women as sisters, with absolute purity.

1 Timothy 5:1–2

Inspirational Insight:

Remember that song, "We Are Family" by Sister Sledge? Yeah, you remember. We all sang, "We are family. I got all my sisters with me. We are family. Get up ev'rybody and sing!" (You're tapping your toes right now, aren't you?)

You know, there's a lot of truth in that little song. Sisterhood is about more than just being related. It's about friendship. It's about empowerment. It's about support. It's about love.

Even if you don't have a blood sister, if you have good friends, you've got it all. Sisters—whether they are sisters in the flesh or sisters in Christ—are gifts from God. Don't ever take them for granted, and determine today to be a Yahweh sister to all of the special women in your life.

Heart to Heaven:

Thank You, Lord, for my sisters. I know that You have given these special women to me, and I treasure the relationship I have with each one—my sister, my sister-in-law, my best friends who seem like sisters, my sisters in Christ—all of them. Father, help me to be the kind of sister, friend, and confidant that will bring glory and honor to Your Name. I love and praise You today. Amen.

Chapter Five

MONUMENTAL MOMENTS:

Sharing Meaningful Adventures

Every desirable and beneficial gift comes out of heaven. The gifts are rivers of light cascading down from the Father of Light. There is nothing deceitful in God, nothing two-faced, nothing fickle.

James 1:17 MSG

Can you remember a monumental moment in your life? One of those moments that you can point to and say, "That's when I changed." Or, "That was the point my life took a turn." Or even simply, "That was a new experience."

Of course, the greatest is the moment we surrender our lives to Christ. Other moments might include marriage, having a child, conquering a fear, or fulfilling a dream.

I remember a moment like that. After working at one company for several years, I had taken another job, in a completely new field. I saw it as a chance to do something new.

It was a big step.

Career-wise, I left behind everything familiar. Unfortunately, it wasn't long before I discovered that I had jumped from the frying pan into the fire. Although I loved my new position, I found that I had no time or energy for anything else—not family, not friends, not church.

As I drove home one day, I got honest with myself. In order to be successful, I knew I would have to live and breathe my new job. I knew I could gain money and prestige from it, but I would lose everything else—family time and peace of mind.

It wasn't worth it.

When I dragged myself through my front door that night, my husband, Chris, a children's author, was there. We sat down and had a heart-to-heart talk. Within three weeks, I had left the job to come home to assist him.

It was a huge step, but looking back, I can see God's hand on the entire situation. If I hadn't left the security of the first company, I would have never had the courage to eventually work from home. Since then, I've seen God's provision everywhere. I thank God for the support of friends and family. They made my monumental moment easier to face.

Think of a moment when your life changed. Can you see God's hand on the situation? Can you see how He sent friends and family to make the moment easier? Whenever we have monumental moments in our lives, we can count on the sure thing—He will never leave us nor forsake us, and He will guide our steps. *GM*

Fire on the Mountain Tonight

Laura L. Smith

The scent of horse clung to me as I walked toward the new barn. I smelled the fresh wood as I neared the still unstained structure, which housed the showers.

"Hey, Chris, wait up!"

I turned my head to see my soul mates at horse camp, Tami and Lauren, jogging up the hill toward me with their duffel bags. As they caught up to me, I wiped my sweaty palms on my jeans, which were speckled with sandy-colored coarse hairs from my horse, Duncan.

"I was looking for you two!"

Lauren rolled her eyes. "Meredith thought we needed to go over the parts of the bridle five more times after we had dismounted."

Our boots clomped up the wooden stairs and into the barn.

"Everyone in my class will get a perfect score on their examination!" mimicked Tami in a nasally voice almost perfectly emulating their riding instructor.

"What are you going to wear tonight?" asked Tami as she removed her silver bracelets.

I pulled the ponytail holder out of my matted hair and listened to Lauren's response. I had stuffed a pair of cut-off jean shorts and a lavender tank with a satin ribbon edge in my duffel, but I had also packed a plain white T-shirt. I was debating over which top to wear to the big campfire. I wanted to look cute since this was our last night at camp, but I didn't want to look too put together for a fire on the mountainside.

This night was about more than looks.

The Final Gathering

After dinner, we hiked up the slope to the week's finale—the campfire on the mountain with the other older campers and their counselors. This was our first year as senior campers, thus our first year to be included in the bonfire ritual.

Lauren stood in the middle with Tami and me on each side of her, arm in arm, singing songs and giggling as we made our ascent.

I smelled the rich smoke of the fire before I saw it.

Several campers had already staked out seats on the large logs serving as benches angled around the bonfire. We walked toward the roaring orange and red flames. Their heat and smoke brought tears to my eyes. Counselors were doling out marshmallows to roast. After cooking and eating our sticky treats, Lauren, Tami, and I settled into seats halfway back from the blaze.

The counselors stood up, one at a time, and told memorable stories from the week. As we clapped and stomped in applause, the guitars started playing.

Music was always my favorite part of each camp day. Although my singing voice was as melodious as a seagull's, I loved to belt out the rhythmic tunes. We sang at the end of every meal, and since Marmon Valley was a Christian camp, we sang Christian songs. I had never known praising God could be so much fun. All of the songs at my pristine church were played on the organ, and the hymnal dated most of them from the 1800s.

The counselors led us in some of our favorites. They sang the verses, and we shouted back the choruses. Then the mood changed. The strumming got softer. What was this next song? I couldn't tell which one it was, yet I was sure I had heard it before.

The smoke from the fire seemed whiter, or was it just easier to see it against the darkening sky? When had the sun gone down? When had the stars come out to light up the evening? I reached out my arms and placed them on Tami's and Lauren's shoulders. Automatically, they put their arms around me, too. We swayed to the soft melody.

No one sang, yet the guitars kept playing this beautiful tune. Then Steve, one of the counselors, stood up. Tami, Lauren, and I all had professed serious crushes on Steve Monday night in our bunks. He was really cute and funny.

"I am a Christian," Steve said. "Four years ago on this very night I dedicated my life to Jesus Christ, and my life has never been the same. We hope your week here has been fun. We hope you have learned a lot about horsemanship and made a lot of friends, but we hope you have experienced something more. We hope you have gotten to know our Lord."

Goosebumps crept up my arms and legs. What was he saying? It felt as if he were speaking directly to me.

The other counselors joined Steve. They all stood in front of us, arm in arm. The music continued, and they began singing softly:

There's a fire on the mountain tonight,

Nowhere to run, nowhere to hide.

We had sung this song all week, but differently. We had sung it loudly and quickly with upbeat verses and strategic hand claps and foot stomps. I had never paused to consider what the lyrics meant.

Steve continued speaking over the soft singing. "I invite any of you here who feel called to invite Jesus as your personal Savior to come forward at this time."

Something tugged at me.

Was anybody really going to go up? Should I go? What did it mean to invite Jesus into my heart? I was already a Christian, wasn't I? I went to church almost every Sunday with my parents. I could never get up in front of this whole group. Were Tami and Lauren going to go up? What would they think if I walked forward…or if I didn't?

As if pulled by a magnet, my body stood without weighing the consequences of its actions. I struggled to sit down before I embarrassed myself, yet my feet moved forward. Cecilia, my riding instructor, reached out to me as I approached the front. She ushered me to a smooth spot on the ground where we sat. The heat of the fire distorted my vision. Everything looked wavy and out of focus.

"Chris," Cecilia almost whispered, her soft hand firmly planted on my back, "do you take Jesus as your personal Savior?"

"I do," the words came out of my mouth.

I was completely unprepared for the emotions that swept over me. My entire body emptied. My whole self just up and left the thirteen-year old girl's frame wearing the cut-off shorts and white T-shirt. I felt a chill and an empty aching as I gasped for air. Then, as quickly as my old being drained, a new self filled me. Tears poured down my face as I was overwhelmed by all of the shame, fear, uncertainty, and insecurity I had ever felt being replaced by pure and beautiful love as I had never experienced.

Cecilia held me, and we rocked.

I don't know how long we sat like that. I lost all sense of time and space. From the moment I knelt on the ground with Cecilia to the time she stood me up was a blur. When had the music stopped? When had the fire burned down to embers? Had anyone else come forward? What had the campers who had remained in their seats done? I didn't have the answers, but it didn't matter.

None of it mattered. I was different. God lived within me. The Holy Spirit had come to dwell in me, and with God's love I could do anything. The things I wanted to do were different, too. I couldn't wait to share my experience with my friends, my family and my world.

My senses somewhat revived, I glanced around for Lauren and Tami. I didn't see Lauren, but Tami walked toward me. I could tell she had prayed the same prayer I had. Her eyes were glowing with His incomparable love.

"Let's go," she whispered.

We made our way toward the mulch path. Tami's arm felt just right around my waist. As we started our descent, we sang together the rest of the chorus,

Tell me, would you be okay, if you had to die today?

There's a fire on the mountain tonight.

And the fire was now in my heart.

Laura L. Smith has published a children's chapter book, *Cantaloupe Trees* (Publish America 2001), as well as had stories appear in *God Allows U-Turns* (Barbour Publishing 2001) and *A Woman's Journey* (Barbour Publishing 2002). She lives in Oxford, Ohio, with her husband and two children.

Heart to Heart:

Describe a monumental moment in your life.

Describe the people who experienced it with you.

Did their presence make the moment more or less memorable?

The Gift of a Moment

S. A. (Shae) Cooke

Lord, help her, I prayed as I walked into the dark bedroom. She sat with her feeble body slumped in the rocking chair. Her pale face tilted to one side. Mother's slightly parted, chalky lips dribbled saliva. Her body, once lithe and agile, was now frail and thin, even against the delicate detail of the chair. I wiped her face and she smiled. Slipping into the chair beside her, I snuggled close, inhaling the familiar scent of the skin I had known from infancy.

This physical closeness is all that remained of the mother-and-daughter relationship we once had. Soon after Mother's diagnosis with Alzheimer's disease, her ability to communicate ceased. Within two years, dementia, a cruel thief, robbed her of the ability to learn, imagine, and reason. Sadly, it advanced rapidly and held her hostage—though without ransom. Our roles reversed, and I became *her* caregiver. My breath caught in my throat as I watched her, and I held back the urge to cry. How I longed to tell her how I loved her and have her understand. It was just too late.

Like the metamorphosis of a butterfly in reverse, she lost her wings—her ability to fly and the personal freedoms she fiercely guarded. Laughter used to resonate throughout the house, echoing her passion and delight in even the smallest things. Now, only weak cries interrupted the heartbreaking silence.

Her milk-white hands clasped a yellowed handkerchief that once belonged to my father. She stared at her fingertips without blinking as they lightly traced the outline of a cursive E embroidered on its corner. Her tears seeped into the kerchief. She kissed it and drew it close.

I laid my head on her chest and closed my eyes for a moment, trying to remember her as she once was.

I am four years old and scrape a knee falling off my tricycle. I run into the house crying and call for my mother. She kneels beside me and looks at the tiny wound. She kisses the damaged spot then holds me close. I smell the familiar scent of lily of the valley on her skin.

Again, I remembered:

It is my wedding day. We are sitting on the bed in my room as she hands me something wrapped with a freshly starched handkerchief. Inside—a string of pearls she wore on her own wedding day. I place them at my throat and lift my hair as she fastens the complicated clasp.

She cups my face with her hands and gently whispers, "Guard your memories and hold them close to your heart, never let them go."

A stream of sunshine filled the room, bringing me back to the present, or *was* it? I felt the warmth of her palms under my chin. Startled, I realized that her eyes, just masked with a veil of tears, were alert and sparkling, brimming with mischief. This was real! We were together in our memories, and now sharing the moment. Our eyes met, and we laughed, delighting in each other's company.

"I love you, Mum," I said. She squeezed my hand and smiled, and then her grip loosened. Her snowy head lifted slightly as her lips formed words without sound. Cradling her in my arms, I hummed her favorite hymn, and as I did, I thought I heard an infant cry. A tear slipped, and I brushed it away as I prayed, "Lord, thank You for giving us one last chance to share our love." God's gift of a final moment would last a lifetime.

S. A. (Shae) Cooke, a Christian freelance writer and mother, lives in Coquitlam, British Columbia.

Reversal

Elizabeth B. Rooney,
submitted by Patricia Rooney Fannon

You were my mother once
And I was child.
You were my mother once,
Omniscient, strong.
Now you have lived so long
I am become
Mother to you
And you, child-like to me.
Yet you are mother still,
Still to be honored, loved,
Shown all respect.
When I was child,
You were kind, brave and true.
May I be such a mother now
To you!

Elizabeth B. Rooney, (BA, Eng. Lit., Smith; MA, Christian Ed., Union Seminary) began writing poetry following a profound encounter with the Holy Spirit. Her poems have appeared in numerous anthologies, magazines, and devotionals. Brigham Farm Publishing recently released *All Miracle,* a four-volume series of Rooney's poetry arranged seasonally.

The 1 + 1 = 3 Principle

Laurie Barker Copeland

You know it when it happens to you. It's almost like an electric charge going through your body.

It's what I call the 1 + 1 = 3 Principle.

My friend, Denise, and I have it.

Denise and I share no activities to bring us together: no carpools, no YMCA, not even church activities. We met when our kids were in preschool together—now they're in separate middle schools. Our homes and our lives are about thirty minutes from each other. What lies between us is a maze of congested traffic, baseball practices, and the day-to-day juggling of families and lives.

Yet when we get together, it's the 1 + 1 = 3 Principle all over again. The funniest things happen and the grandest of things happen. When we brainstorm, thoughts that were log-jammed become unclogged and ideas start flowing. As we talk, we share our concerns, and monumental problems become smaller. The 1 + 1 = 3 Principle creates a chemistry between two people, causing them to accomplish much more than they would separately.

I believe it's this principle that God inspired the author of Ecclesiastes to write about, in the fourth chapter of that book: "Though one may be overpowered, two can defend themselves. A cord of three strands is not quickly broken" (verse 12). This verse obviously applies to marriage, but it also can apply to friendships. When God is the focus of our hearts and conversations, He works even when we're not aware of it.

The most memorable example of this 1 + 1 = 3 Principle occurred when Denise's family of five and my family of three waited outside a stadium for a political rally to begin. Along with seven thousand other people, we stood together like an overstuffed box of matchsticks.

It had already been a long, hot wait. Our feet were tired; our bodies were sweaty; and our moods were cranky. (And those were just the adults!) Denise and I decided that singing would help pass the time, so we began our repertoire with "God Bless America." (Neither Denise nor I would have ever begun a song on our own.) But together, we knew that the other would pick up the tune before the second note escaped from our mouth.

First our kids began singing, and then our spouses and neighbors joined in. Very soon, the thousands packed in around us sang, the melody swaying back and forth through the breeze. The volume rose and swelled as if it were being led by the Divine Conductor.

Within a split second, irritable people transformed into a unified, reverent body. Like a flame on a single candle touching another candle, our song had spread to thousands within seconds.

> Though one may be overpowered, two can defend themselves. A cord of three strands is not quickly broken. (Ecclesiastes 4:12.) This verse obviously applies to marriage, but it also can apply to friendships.
>
> —Laurie Barker Copeland

Denise and I looked at each other, as if to say, "What just happened here?" We both had tears in our eyes. We had both felt it: The 1 + 1 = 3 Principle.

Was this sudden change of the crowd's mood because of Denise's and my virtuoso singing qualities? Hardly. We can sing on tune, but our voices are nothing to write home about. No, the group's change of attitude was because God flowed through two friends that stood stronger together than apart.

I love it when God works like that! He took a humid night, a group of grouchy, sweaty people, and two friends' spontaneous singing, and turned it into one of life's "God moments."

Laurie Barker Copeland is a speaker, humorist, actress and shower singer. She is co-author of *The Groovy Chicks Road Trip to Peace* and *The Groovy Chicks' Road Trip to Love*, and is a contributor for *Caution: Children Praying; Humor for the Teacher's Heart; But Lord, I Was Happy Shallow; Your Spiritual Personality* and other books. She holds Girlfriend Getaway women's retreats and her latest adventure is playing the part of "Pepper" with The Groovy Chicks at women's conferences. Her favorite production performs daily at her Orlando home with her husband, John, and daughter, Kailey, who are constant sources of material for Laurie's stories.

Up Close and Personal:

Describe another monumental moment in your life. How did you see God's hand in that moment? What did you learn through that time?

Perfect Plan

Vicki Fisher-Wellnitz

Call me a control freak! I prefer to use the word *planner*. It probably started in my childhood, but I recognized it during high school. My plan was this: Go to college, then move to Southern California and begin a career in the entertainment industry. Down the line I would get married, have children, and continue with my career. I had many other goals along the way, of course, as all planners do. And although it hasn't been a straight path—there have been curves thrown in here and there—I have kept pretty much to my "plan."

I had always dreamed of traveling to Europe. And I wanted to do it before my husband and I had children. People said to me, "Why don't you wait until your retirement to take this trip?" But I wanted to experience it now! It was on my list of "Things To Do Before We Have Children." So, we traveled to Europe. It was amazing! It changed my life—seeing other parts of the world and how others lived, and that there are actually buildings older than 200 years that still exist today!

The next plan on my list, after we returned home from our travels, was to start our family. We had gone to Europe in April; if we got pregnant in May, we'd have a February baby. A perfect plan!

A perfect plan in my eyes, but not so in God's.

I did not get pregnant in May or June or July or even August. My "plan" was not on track. Questions popped into my mind from, "When would I get pregnant?" to "Would I ever have children of my own?" Relatives and friends around me were having children—no problem. At the time, stories of infertility and miscarriage were few and far between, at least to my ears. My husband has a daughter from a previous relationship, so I thought he should be capable. What's wrong with me? I wanted a child so badly! It wasn't just a part of my "plan"; my heart longed for a child. And now I was crying out to God for this blessing. But why hadn't it come? I was so ready for this addition to our family, why wasn't it arriving? After all of our fertility tests, the results showed that my husband and I were healthy and normal.

We had family and friends encircling us in prayer. I even talked my husband into coming to my women's Bible study, so that my friends could pray over us together. I thought I was doing all the "right" things.

> I instantly had to turn to God and let go of the reins. This is God's timing and God's plan. He has the ultimate road map.
>
> —Vicki Fisher-Wellnitz

Then one of my friends said to me, "Vicki, you've planned everything out in your life like a road map. God is showing you, it's not your plan, but His. You have to lean on and trust in Him."

I've always prayed, but I've never totally surrendered myself to the Lord. I realized that this wasn't on my watch any longer; this was God's timing. I surrendered myself and put all of my trust in the Lord. Now this is hard to do for a control freak—uh, planner.

Isaiah 30:15 says, "In quietness and trust is your strength."

The Lord answered my every prayer. I did get pregnant in May and had a February baby—it was just a year later. And the more I spoke to other women, the more I realized how blessed we were. It only took us one year to conceive, while many others have had to struggle much longer, and go down the tough road of dealing with infertility.

When I look back on the year before I became pregnant, I see that both my relationship with the Lord and my relationship with my husband grew stronger. So many of our loved ones prayed for us, and those prayers were answered in so many ways. When we first tried to conceive, we lived in an apartment, that for certain reasons, was not a safe, relaxing refuge anymore. Later, we were able to buy a condo in a wonderful community, and we were in a better place financially. I could go on and on with a list of everything that fell into place over the next two years, before we had our son. It was all on God's time, it was just a matter of me surrendering to and trusting Him.

I still have a plan for my life, although it's changed drastically in the last couple of years. I could not have imagined how wonderful it's turning out with God leading the way. I've hit the hard places where I cling tightly to my way, but God is there gently loosening my grip. "We can make our plans, but the LORD determines our steps" (Proverbs 16:9 NLT).

So, here my husband and I are, again. Our son just turned two, and we started trying for another child five months ago. Of course, it was natural (as a planner) to start mapping things out: If we start at this time, we'll have a baby born at this time, and the baby will be old enough to go on the next spring vacation.... (See what I mean about planning?)

I instantly had to turn to God and let go of the reins. This is God's timing and God's plan. He has the ultimate road map. He might bless us with another child next year or maybe the next. Or, He may have other plans for me, and I will never stop thanking the Lord for the blessings of my son and my stepdaughter. For now, I leave it in His hands. He knows what's best. He knows the best route for me on His road map.

My strength will come in my quietness and trust in Him.

He has a perfect plan for me!

Vicki Fisher-Wellnitz and her husband, Mike, of 10 years, recently moved from Orange County, California, back to their hometown, Rushville, Nebraska. They have two sons, Zackary, 4½ and Jacob, 1½. Mike's daughter, Lindsay, 13, lives in Elk Grove, California. Vicki works part time in the investment department of their local bank.

An Honor Beyond Measure

Michelle Shocklee

Friendships come and sometimes go.
I'm thankful ours has stayed.
There are times it's difficult to love,
And there are times we disagree.
But ours is one of the special kind
That holds together, come what may.

Your life has changed more so than mine
With your new baby that arrived last May.
I thought we were all through with babies and births
And were preparing for empty nests.
But God had other plans, you see,
And filled your arms once again.

The day your daughter came into the world
Is written on my heart.
The miracle of life I saw emerge
Was more awesome than words can tell.
Through tears of joy you smiled at me
And spoke her name aloud.
"Arabella Michelle" you said with love,
An honor beyond measure.

Friendships come and sometimes go.
I'm thankful ours has stayed.
We'll always be connected now,
Through a beautiful life that grows each day.
From your heart to mine,
From mine to yours,
God wanted it that way.

Michelle Shocklee is happily married with two wonderful sons. She is also a freelance writer, having written devotionals, articles, and several novels. Her dear friend, Amy, honored her beyond measure last May by naming her beautiful little daughter after her. It was the most humbling moment of her life.

Celebrate the Moment:

Grab some girlfriends and enjoy a monumental moment—attend an art gallery for the first time, throw your first annual barbeque or party, join a health club together and take the first step toward getting in shape—anything that you can one day reflect on and say: "That was something worth remembering; that was a monumental moment."

Intimate Details:

The steps of a good man are ordered by the Lord: and he delighteth in his way. Though he fall, he shall not be utterly cast down: for the Lord upholdeth him with his hand.

Psalm 37:23–24 KJV

Trust in the Lord with all your heart and lean not on your own understanding.

Proverbs 3:5

Inspirational Insight:

Isn't it comforting to know that while we live here on earth, our heavenly Father steadily guides our lives? The scriptures in this chapter, James 1:17, Psalm 37:23–24, and Proverbs 3:5, are wonderful reminders of that.

We have a personal heavenly Father who loves each of us through all of our monumental moments—the good and the bad. He hasn't abandoned us or merely watched us from afar. No, He's given us His Son to intercede for us, His Holy Spirit to comfort and direct us, and a divine sisterhood to be His tangible hands and feet.

Sometimes when challenges come, we want to take the reins. We want to control or, as Vicki Fisher-Wellnitz puts it, *plan* the things that happen to us. (Can anyone say "amen" to that?) But the greatest step we can take is to surrender our lives, and our futures, to Him.

He knows what's best for us.

As Psalm 37 reminds us, He's already got the path marked. All we have to do is follow Him down it.

Heart to Heaven:

Lord, thank You for guiding the steps of my life. And thank You for sending friends and family to walk the path with me. Help me to take the time to invite You into every moment of my life and to remember that You are with me through all the good and bad. Amen.

Chapter Six

WIND BENEATH MY WINGS:

Celebrating Our Mothers

As a mother comforts her child, so I'll comfort you.

Isaiah 66:13 MSG

They've tucked us into warm beds, snuggled with us on their laps, and soothed away our fears after bad dreams. They've believed in us through dance recitals, high school speeches, and college graduations. They're our mothers, and celebrating them is easy to do.

They're an amazing group.

I myself have two very different, equally beautiful mothers. One I was born to; the other I inherited.

My own mother is hands-down the hardest working, most independent person I know. She can cook as easily for twenty as she can for four, and she is just as comfortable in boots while watching her horses gallop at the track, as she is at a dinner party in three-inch heels.

My other mother, the one whom I was blessed enough to inherit when I wisely married her son, is a mom in the sweetest sense of the word. She has a witty sense of humor—I never tire of hearing her chuckle at one of life's ironies—and her tins of Christmas cookies are a favorite year after year.

Both of these graceful women have added to my life. Aside from birthing, raising, teaching, and loving me, they have—more importantly—

shared their faith with me. And of all the gifts a mother can give, isn't that the most precious?

As you read through these stories and poems celebrating mothers, hopefully you'll be reminded of the beautiful lessons your mother, or another mother figure, shared with you. *GM*

By Way of the Angels

Caroline Honn

She *knows.*
Our love is more
than bear hugs and Hallmark cards, more
than plane tickets and books and homemade jams all
packed together on the same day in
one giant priority mail box.

She knows we love more
than words, more than tears,
more than time.

It is so through
her love for us—
unbound, timeless, too large
for life itself to comprehend
but through the God who made us.

She knows we love her big;
and the word *goodbye* wasn't an option—
not while there were loved ones to visit and little doll clothes to make,
not while there was still "stuff" to talk about.
She's in and out of our consciousness,
in and out of our breath as we absorb the realization that
she's in our hearts now more profoundly than ever.
Knowing this will need to be enough
until we meet again to celebrate forever.
By way of the angels—we love her big.

Caroline Honn lives with her husband and three children in Arizona, where she works as a freelance writer. "There is nothing more fulfilling than experiencing the transformation of suffering and loss into a profound sense of the real God in our lives. A mother's love goes far beyond this world."

Heart to Heart:

Describe your mother in one or two words.

What have you learned from your mother?

When you think of your mother, what immediately comes to your mind? A special memory? A piece of advice?

It's Not about Rocks

Leslie J. Wyatt

Somewhere in the high desert country of southwestern Utah, lost along the edge of an endless wheat field, stands a porch. A rock porch, solid as the ground from which it came. Once there was a house there, too—with gray gravel siding, peeling white window trim, and hollyhocks splashing purples and pinks and whites bravely along one side.

There, where rain rarely fell and sagebrush formed the only lawn, the little house was home to a mother with an eye for beauty and a courage that was kin to the land itself. While her husband wrestled a living out of the long fields of wheat and pinto beans, she pushed back the dust and the dryness and courted color in the midst of grays and dusty greens.

At first, the little house had a rickety porch of weathered gray wood. Then one day, the mother took a battered red wagon and five little kids, and hauled load after load of rust and gold rocks from the edge of the field, from the side of the road, from the floor of the pinyon and juniper woods. Slowly, the pile grew. And then one day, this mother began to build.

She mixed cement batch by batch. Course by course, she laid the stones, hefting them, turning them, fitting them. Layer by layer she taught herself the art of stonework. Foot by foot, the porch grew alongside the house, and she laid broad, gracious steps to the peeling white door. Finally, the last stone was placed on the floor of the porch, and the mother and her children could stand on the monument to her bravery and gaze off across the waving green wheat.

Season followed season. The children grew. The family moved. The hollyhocks disappeared. Then one sad day the little gray house burned to the ground. Today, only the porch remains. To those who happen by, it is a block of stone, something to be walked around, wondered about, ignored.

But almost four decades later, in a valley in western Montana under the towering shadow of the blue Mission Mountains, is a rock garden. It is a place of delight, where water cascades down in succeeding splashes, to plunge into a rock-encircled pool set about with water-loving plants that capture the colors of a painter's palette. Another mother bends over her creation, adjusting this stone, tending that plant. Behind her rings the laughter of *her* children.

And beside an old white farmhouse on the edge of the rolling Ozarks in west-central Missouri, rock pathways meander through flowerbeds ablaze with blues, reds, and the colors of summer. The walkways lead through the scent of lavender and pinks, and the fragile blushing tenacity of a bank of Missouri Primrose. Yet another mother repositions migrating stone, and redefines the end of a path, and the hands of *her* children take part in the process.

All those long years ago, when that first mother—my mother—gathered up her courage and hauled wagonload after wagonload of stones to fashion a porch, she didn't know she was also building into the hearts and hands of her children something as solid and enduring as the porch itself. Perhaps she saw no farther than the need for a more stable, more beautiful entrance to her home, but through the undertaking of the project, she nonetheless empowered our lives by her bravery.

Sometimes when I feel discouraged that I have made no impact on the world as I once aspired to do, and wonder if I'll leave anything lasting behind me, I remember my mother. I smell again the sagebrush and dust as I watched her build the old stone porch. I think of my sister's rock garden, cool, colorful, and full of beauty, and gaze out the window at my own rock pathways as they meander through my flower garden. Then I look at my own children and I smile.

Leslie J. Wyatt is a homeschooling mom and freelance writer for children and adults. Her husband, Dave, and she have been blessed with six children, and they live in Missouri on a "sort-of" farm with chickens, garden, dog, and cats, and more than their fair share of mice.

Old Flowerpots and Other Junk

M. Kathryn Gray

It was Christmas 1964, and I was fourteen years old. Dad had gone to find a suitable Christmas tree. We lived in the country, and unlike city-folk who bought beautiful firs, our farm provided us a common cedar each year. A cold blast of wind gushed through the door as Dad kicked it open, carrying a large tree into the room.

"Do you think this will do?" he asked.

Without saying a word, I thought, *Why can't we ever buy a fir?*

It seemed to me that we never had anything like everyone else. Mother opened the box of ornaments. The shiny paint was chipping off the balls, the foil tinsel was crushed and coming off the string that held it together, and the paper ornaments were tattered and worn. We even used the same old icicles from year to year, bent and crooked. The bubble lights annoyingly gurgled as they bubbled! Sometimes, we strung popcorn into long strings to hang on the tree. Homemakers today would have loved our tree, calling it "vintage."

"Would you rather I spend money on ornaments and a tree and not give you any gifts?" my mother responded whenever I complained.

Everyone else had color-coordinated ornaments and the most modern of lights with beautifully wrapped packages beneath their trees. So, why couldn't we?

A Giving Nature

Our kitchen always smelled of the fresh-baked cookies, breads, and candies that my mother made for us and for neighbors and friends.

"Want to go with me in a few minutes?" she asked.

I knew she was going to make deliveries to our aged neighbors who lived near our farm.

"I guess so," I answered, knowing she would talk with our neighbors and eventually I would have to beg her to come home.

Mother has always loved people and has given a great deal of her time to help others. She has always been especially drawn to broken and lonely people. I remember she often took food to an old alcoholic derelict who lived in a rundown shack near the railroad tracks because no one in our little community went without a Christmas treat if she knew of a need.

> Most people would have thrown it in the trash, but Mother is a visionary. She sees value in the valueless.
>
> —M. Kathryn Gray

My mother had grown up during the Great Depression when there was very little to go around. Living with her grandmother, she learned to appreciate even the smallest gift. Once, she received a mere hair ribbon for her Christmas gift, and many Christmases, there was no gift at all. In those days people often gave food as gifts. There were egg-less cakes and meat-less pies. There was sugar-free candy before it was ever trendy. People were poor. Spices and such were scarce, so they used what they had and created from them as best they could. In spite of their poverty, people had good hearts and gave to one another.

Love in the Purest Form

Today, when I visit Mother, I can't help but notice things sitting around that I consider junk: wheels, buckets, old hardware, doors, broken furniture, glass objects, tin, and metal. Her porch is lined with cracked and chipped flowerpots and some are not even flowerpots at all. It is not unusual to see an object of questionable value sitting near her garage work area.

"Mother, what are you going to do with this?" I ask.

Then she explains that she will attach another object to it, put some handles on here or there, paint it, and voilà, a snack table! She has a knack for fixing and repairing worn-out items. She enjoys working with her hands, creating something from nothing.

I remember a beautiful ceramic angel that had broken into many pieces. She painstakingly glued it back together. She filled the cracks with a paste until you could hardly tell it had been broken. She added a pretty bow to cover a spot that was irreparable. Once again, the angel stood tall and glorious! Most people would have thrown it in the trash, but Mother is a visionary. She sees value in the valueless.

Her life was broken in many ways, growing up without the mother, father, or home she longed for. As a young woman, God called her to minister to children. Today she still teaches young boys and girls in her church about the precious love of Jesus. Some of those children have become pastors and teachers themselves.

She pieces together broken objects, shares them with her friends and family, changing the lives of others through her care and love for the brokenhearted, the lonely, and the needy in her community. If asked why she spends so much time on useless junk, she will tell you it's to earn extra money. However, as I observe her life, I see her giving away more than she sells. Through giving, she introduces herself to people in need. As she does, she is loved and serves God by telling people in distress about the love of Jesus. Young and old alike look to her for spiritual guidance.

Her home is not "beautiful" as many people think of beauty, but it is warm and loving. When I see a new piece of junk in her shop, I wonder what fortunate person is going to be the recipient of Jesus' love. Now, when I think of those old Christmas ornaments, my heart is blessed to know that my mother has known love in its purest form—by giving.

Mary Kathryn Gray, who resides in Fort Worth, Texas, began writing inspirational works in 1995. Awarded the International Poet of Merit Award for Outstanding Contribution to the Art of Poetry, her poem, "My Daily Creed, Just One More Day" is published in three anthologies. She has two sons, a daughter-in-law, and two grandchildren.

Shackled

(Initiated response of "Sweet Release" by Diane M. O'Neal)

Brandy S. Brow

I sought, I searched, I did not find,

but eventually I yearn to honor the one in whose hands
God entrusted my life.

You say you faltered, you failed, you did not teach,

but look at me now and who I've become;
no failure is out of God's reach.

We laughed, we cried, we argued a lot,

but through all the years God taught me to remember
only the love you brought.

Now we laugh, we cry, we encourage each other,

sisters in the Lord, friends, yet shackled daughter and mother.

Now I ask, I plead, I do not lie,

will you please forgive yourself all the wrongs
you think you've done in my life?

You withdraw, you retreat, you give no reprieve,

but what the devil meant to harm you and I, God used for good in me.

We would've laughed, cried, argued in vain,

if God had never used our mistakes before to teach while we live today.

Please may we laugh, cry, encourage each other,

sisters in the Lord, friends, and liberated daughter and mother?

Talking with Mom, I used to hit walls of regret and shame from her perception that she had failed as my mother. I longed for those walls to be gone so we could build a strong, adult relationship. That's when I wrote "Shackled." **Brandy S. Brow**

Up Close and Personal:

Describe your relationship with your mother. Has it been good? Challenging? Why? Describe her—her hopes, dreams, strengths, weaknesses.

Sweet Release

(Response to "Shackled" by Brandy S. Brow)

Diane M. O'Neal

Born a message of love, you're His gift from above.
Oh, how my mother's heart sought to excel.
God, however, allowed life as it was;
'midst my imperfections, far short I fell.

All the things done—or left undone—
would mar you for life, I was *sure.*
I'd forgotten that God, who's above all and one,
is forever through all we endure.

Individually journeying closer to Him,
over time allowed us to see,
He is faithful to bring us past places so grim,
and HEALED—yes, in spite of me!

Where I was bound, where I was caught,
you heard grief-filled guilt, saw anguish-filled shame.
Your forgiving heart freed me when my condemning heart could not,
with loving forgiveness you refused to lay blame.

You took on Christ's likeness on my behalf
choosing to see only what is new and good,
For you offered me love when I offered me wrath;
you yearned to move beyond. Oh, if only I would.

My joyful heart bursts with this message to send:
those shackles which separated, restricted, and bound,
My sister in the Lord, my daughter, my friend,
have loosed, vanished, are nowhere found!

Now, more clearly, we begin to understand
how Christ's forgiveness of sin sets captives free.
For, likewise, as we offer forgiveness' healing hand,
there—reconciled—is the freedom for love between me and thee.

My daughter's message was clear; she desired a relationship with me woman-to-woman, heart-to-heart. What a blessing! I longed for the same, not knowing the lies I believed were in the way. My 'walls of regret' needed to come down. "Sweet Release" let her know. **Diane M. O'Neal**

Independence Taught and Caught

Sharon Norris Elliott

My mother, Nancy Norris, wanted to raise independent children and avoid becoming a burden on us once we were grown. She desired always to be a welcome face in our lives. When we moved out of the house and got married, she waited for our invitation to visit and refused to barge in unexpectedly. When she did call us, she asked to make sure she wasn't interrupting our time with our spouses. She even chose appropriate gifts, never giving something we hated but had to use or display simply because they came from Mother.

This hands-off policy worked well, and she stuck with it. Once Mom retired from teaching and Dad no longer preached every Sunday, they carried on their independent lives as a couple, never seeming to suffer any empty-nest syndrome. In fact, they kept so busy, it was hard to catch up with them sometimes, even for babysitting.

"You've got to phone me at least a week in advance and make a reservation," Mom might tell me, "because your father and I will probably have a church dinner or choir concert lined up to attend."

I found out just how independent Mom expected me to be when I had my first son. All was wonderful when the family visited the hospital and saw that newborn Matthew and I were all right. But the moment I got him home, he started to cry and refused to stop. I fed him, changed him, rocked him, and gave him a pacifier. Nothing worked. I called Mom. She came right over, looked at Matthew, and asked, "What's wrong with him?"

"You're the one with the experience," I teased, "you tell me."

"Oh no," she countered. "How do you think I got the experience? You will figure him out. See you in two weeks. We're off to the national church convention." And with that, Mom was out the door and on her way with Dad across the country. Of course, I did figure Matthew out and I got through those first weeks with my new baby just fine, as Mom had predicted.

After Dad died, Mom remained independent, as she'd always taught us to be. She'd drive herself to all of her functions, picking up her best friend, Miss Gussie, on the way. We couldn't get Mom to move into the twenty-first century and carry a cell phone, either. She'd say, "If I want you to know where I am, I'll tell you."

Then one day, she called me to say she wasn't feeling too well and needed me to accompany her to the doctor. She drove to my house, and I drove her to the clinic. The doctor didn't like what he saw in the examination so he admitted her. The next day, they found a cancerous tumor. Before the week was out, surgeons removed the tumor and half of her stomach with it.

> Mom had always supported us, but she realized the importance of stepping aside, allowing us to mature and learn to depend on God.
>
> —Sharon Norris Elliott

Mom was never the same. The subsequent chemotherapy sapped her energy and diminished her appetite. Now ill and living with my sister, her independent streak caused her to feel like a burden. There was no way that was true. Because Mom had taught us to care for ourselves, we had the love and the strength to care for her. In fact, it was an honor. Caring for her also pointed our faces and our faith toward God. We came to realize that times will come when, as independent as we are, we will have to lean on the love of others.

God was there for Mom as she independently strolled into His arms in the early-morning hours of March 17, 2001. She left us a note with such detailed instructions about handling her affairs, that by two that afternoon, all that was left for us to do was comfort one another. Mom had always supported us, but she realized the importance of stepping aside, allowing us to mature and learn to depend on God. She knew He could be with us when she couldn't. My brother, sister, and I were able to deliver Mom's eulogy to the standing-room-only crowd because Mom had taught us how to stand on our own, with God at our side.

Sharon Norris Elliott is an author and popular speaker whose messages touch the hearts of her audiences at conferences, retreats, and other functions. She also teaches high school English and journalism at a Christian school in Inglewood, California, near where she, her husband, James, and their two teenage sons live.

Bargain Hunter

Valerie J. Frost

"Your mama is the only one I know who can shop for four hours, and then when she comes home and you ask her what she bought, she says…'Nothing.'" My father joked, but he knew my mother's shopping expeditions were quite serious. Though he put on a pretty good show of teasing her, he heartily approved and appreciated her tenacious efforts to stretch those hard-earned paychecks.

Mom has the knack of stumbling onto spectacular bargains. This has served as a handy gift to me as a working mother with a family of my own. It's a known fact that when I really need something and need to pinch pennies, all I have to do is mention it.

"Mom, will you keep an eye out for that when you're looking through the ads or at the store, and if you see it on sale, let me know?"

Like the time the dog ate our electric blanket cord and the manufacturer wanted me to pay $30 for a new set of controls. As quick as I could say "discount price," she locked onto the best bargain in town, and I got a call.

"I just happened to be at the linen outlet store today. You know that king-sized electric blanket you were looking for? Well, it was 50 percent off the regular price and I had another 25-percent discount coupon on top of that. It was $49.95, and I couldn't pass it up. All they had was burgundy (my favorite color), but if you don't like it, you can take it back."

Yeah right—fat chance of that happening!

I admire her ability to get terrific prices on almost anything. She finds a table of markdown designer shoes, regular price $100—one pair left, her size, and she pays a whopping $3. I, on the other hand, poke forlornly through a huge pile of exquisite looking and terrifically priced shoes, searching frantically for my size seven, only to find the whole table filled with size twelves.

I've always joked, truthfully, that when the sales clerks see my mom coming down the aisle toward the 75-percent markdown rack, they run up and grab the merchandise from her hand, yelling insistently, "Please…let me mark that down for you another 50 percent!"

As for me, when I enter the store, bells and whistles obviously alert all available clerks to immediately destroy any markdown sign and raise the price on any item that might draw my attention. I don't need to say that I desperately need a shopping intercessor. That's my mom, and believe me, she's been responsible for getting me some pretty good stuff.

Molding the Gifts

Though I don't seem to have her knack for getting bargains, I have tried to learn from her example. I'm not sure how she got so good at what she does, but I think it has to do with sacrifice and learning to persevere through hard times. She went through the Depression with her parents, and she saw what it took to get along in those difficult times.

Then, surviving life as a young wife of an alcoholic wasn't easy, either, especially when there were three children to feed on what was left from the paycheck that wasn't spent at the bar or handed over to bill collectors. And it wasn't easy for a young divorcée, who hadn't been allowed to work, to get a job and support those children alone. But she did, and I don't remember going hungry or doing without anything I needed. When she remarried, my stepdad knew that he had found a precious jewel.

I think God uses the difficult times of our lives to mold the gifts that we have. I thank God for my mother, for her perseverance, her love, and her example of faith. From my observations and experience, my mom has been that godly example of the Proverbs 31 woman, who works hard, loves, and sacrifices for her family, and perceives that her merchandise is good.

Spotting the Deal

One spectacular day in San Diego, California, at the Balboa Park Organ Pavilion, I was with my mom as we listened to a Good Friday message about love, sacrifice, and provision. It talked about our God and His Son, who sacrificed everything for the needs of those He loves. There was no way we could pay the price for what we needed most desperately—a Savior. As the message closed, my mom sat on the edge of her seat, and the invitation to come forward had barely rolled out of our pastor's mouth when she stood up and turned to me without breaking stride. "Want to go up with me?"

> I'm not sure how she got so good at what she does, but I think it has to do with sacrifice and learning to persevere through hard times.
>
> —Valerie J. Frost

I didn't need to think about that one.

We breezed past the clapping crowd, the first ones to reach the platform. Moments later I had the privilege of witnessing my mother publicly acknowledge and accept Jesus Christ as her Lord and Savior. There was no prouder moment in my life except maybe watching her be baptized several months later on our trip to Israel.

I've prayed long and hard for my friends and family. Sometimes I worry or become discouraged about their salvation, fearing that I'm not always the best example, but trying desperately to be genuine and not pushy or religious when I talk about my own relationship with Christ. But God keeps showing me that He has a plan...and His plans are perfect.

Our heavenly Father knows each of us intimately. He knew my mother before she was created, what she would be like, and what she would do. God knew her struggles, her weaknesses, and her strengths. And He planned that, even in a world full of deceit, false hope, and broken promises, she would find the most excellent way.

A Father's perfect love, His Son's sacrifice, and the free gift of eternal life that cleared her path to the glorious streets of gold—that was something she couldn't refuse. There was no doubt she'd make the right choice. After all, Mom knows quality when she sees it, and she can always spot a bargain.

Valerie J. Frost is a freelance writer and an office manager for the facilities department at Horizon Christian Fellowship, in San Diego, California. She and her husband, Terry, are parents of three grown children. They have seven energetic grandchildren, and a turbo-charged Jack Russell terrier named Rocket.

Celebrate the Moment:

Even if it's not Mother's Day, send a card, letter, e-mail, or gift to your mother or a mother figure in your life. Tell her what she means to you. Even if she has passed away, take a moment to write her a letter expressing how she touched you.

Unconditional Love

Ruth Mark

You put champ on the table
a glistening mound of white potato
golden-topped, sprouting green.
Or, you had a pot of jam on the go
the aroma filling the house
with a sticky sweetness, your apron
splashed bloody, a basin of shiny
black jewels ready for the next batch
on the scrubbed Formica work-top.
Food prepared with love
eaten with—we never went hungry
were clothed thanks to your expertise
with the needle, warm, snug—
you'd joke you'd knit us a man
when we were hormone-raging teenagers.
Everything was comforting, a close-knit family unit
us against the world, difficult to
cope when she flew the nest
and found people "out there" were not
like us. Ironically they don't really
begin to talk, until she fell from the invisibly
erected, pedestal, the eldest daughter's
path gone awry, hitting dead-ends
cages every-which-way she turned
salvation at the end of a phone line
but most of all, the soul-deep knowledge
that you were there, always there
your unconditional love a gift
she finally embraced.

Ruth Mark is a licensed psychologist and freelance writer. Originally from Northern Ireland, she currently lives in the Netherlands. She has also lived in Scotland and in France. Her work has been published in diverse print and web venues including *Riviera Reporter*, *Dakota House Journal*, and *Poems Niederngasse*.

My Mother in Me

Stacy Smith

I watch her, without her knowing
I see her so objectively now
A woman with a past, with hopes and dreams
And suddenly I think I understand how
Amazing life is, passed from one to another
Conceived in a moment of bliss
A baby, a life, a creation of two
And it all started with a look, and a kiss

I realize that, from the day I was born
I've unintentionally adopted her ways
Her humor, how to always be a lady
And I'll thank her for the rest of my days
Her selfless giving, her unlimited love
Giving me wings and letting me fly
Respecting people, loving myself
These are lessons I'll carry through life

I see her smiling, I have her eyes
And I see in us, a common air
How we hold ourselves, how we react
to situations…she suddenly returns my stare
And just for a moment, I feel I am
Looking at time—at mothers of mothers before
Each with her own story, a different tale
For all our daughters, forevermore.

Stacy Smith is a freelance writer from her home in the mountains of Colorado. She travels the world extensively and writes for corporations and small businesses, and is also working on several books and screenplays.

Intimate Details:

Respect your father and mother—God, your God, commands it! You'll have a long life; the land that God is giving you will treat you well.

Deuteronomy 5:16 MSG

Inspirational Insight:

Mother. The word alone brings to mind images of warmth and security, wisdom and strength. These wonderful women worked tirelessly to help us become the best we can be. They are our role models, comforters, encouragers and examples of how to walk through life—even in high heels.

Who among us can't attest to learning valuable lessons from them? Their lessons range from how to make the flakiest piecrust to how to stay strong in the face of adversity. In time, hopefully, we'll grow up to be just like them. Then we can pass on their wit and wisdom to the next generation—our children. And the tradition will continue.

If, however, your relationship with your mother has been strained, or non-existent, ask God to direct you to someone who can be a spiritual mother to you, someone who can give you the motherly support that each of us needs. If you need to forgive your mother, ask God to show you how to give and receive that freedom—and yes, forgiveness *always* brings freedom. Don't live in the shadow of an unhealthy upbringing. Instead, live it honoring God, the One who loves you more than anyone else.

So, whether you honor your maternal mother, or a spiritual mother that God has placed in your life, remember she is a blessing from God. Then make a quality decision to bless her—in thought and in deed—every day.

Heart to Heaven:

Lord, thank You for my mother. I pray that she would feel Your love today. Help me remember and respect that as much as she is (or was) my mother, she is also Your child. Help me to see her as You do—with the same love and grace. Amen.

Chapter Seven

MOTHERS' REFLECTIONS:

Precious Gifts from God

All your children shall be taught by the Lord, and great shall be the peace of your children.

Isaiah 54:13 NKJV

"Well, I just wouldn't sit by her at lunch anymore," I said matter-of-factly as I brushed my ten-year-old daughter's hair into a pony-tail. "If that little girl is causing that much trouble within your group of friends, I would simply avoid her."

Abby listened as I continued on my path of parental wisdom.

"And furthermore, if she continues to say ugly things to you, I will go to your teacher and make sure you are never in a situation where you have to sit next to her again."

By this time, Allyson, my eight-year-old, had joined us, listening to every word.

Neither of my daughters interrupted as I finished my heartfelt speech, filled with nuggets of motherly insight.

Then, as I was spritzing each of them with my latest Bath & Body Works fragrance, Allyson's words of wisdom emerged from a haze of Sun-Ripened Raspberry.

"Mom," she said. "I was just thinking. Maybe Abby is supposed to be that girl's friend so that she can witness to her. Maybe Abby is supposed to let that girl see Jesus through her."

Ouch.

Yep, I had become the student. And in that moment, I realized that just because I wear the "Mother Hat," that certainly didn't make me right all of the time. In fact, at that moment I wanted to pull that hat over my face and hide.

How could I have been so "off" on this one? I wondered.

"Yes, that's a good point," I commented, forcing a half smile at my girls. "Abby, you handle this situation the way you feel God would want you to, and I'll be praying for you."

"OK," she said, giving me a quick hug before bolting out the door and off to school.

"See ya, Mom!" Allyson called, following her big sister out the door.

I was left alone—in my bunny slippers—to pray and ponder.

In those following quiet moments, I asked the Lord to forgive my harsh tongue where that little girl was concerned, and I thanked Him for giving me two remarkable daughters—little in stature but big in heart.

Our children have great lessons to teach us—if we'll only listen. *MMA*

My Daughter, My Friend

Micki Roberts

Small and helpless, you entered my life
You wrapped yourself around my
Heart and held on tight
—My daughter, my baby.
As you grew so grew my love for you.
How is it possible to love more every day,
Yet love you more every day I do.
I love your laughter, your hugs and smiles.
I love your generosity and your tender heart
—My daughter, my child.
I feared your teenage years
But you were so open, so willing to talk
And so willing to listen
You allowed me to guide you
You allowed me to make mistakes.
You allowed me to ask for forgiveness
And you always gave it.
You gave so much of yourself to me.
You taught me so much
—My daughter, my teacher.
Now you are a young woman.
How I have loved to watch you
Become the person you are now.
God, in His infinite wisdom
Placed you in my life
To show me how much He loves me

And to teach me how to love.
I thank you for the laughter
For the wonderful times we've shared.
I thank you for the hugs
Just when I need them the most.
I love you and I thank you
For loving me.
—My daughter, my friend

Micki Roberts works part-time in a Baptist association office. She and her husband have two grown children and they reside in Florida. Micki writes novels, devotions, poetry, and lyrics.

My Little Angel

Karen Frost Underwood

As I sat at the kitchen table, I couldn't stop the tears from flowing. *What am I going to do with another child?* I thought.

I wasn't married and didn't want to get married just because I was pregnant.

This is what happens when you don't do things God's way, I thought.

After a long pregnancy, Lora was born in October 1992. She was a beautiful baby—almost angelic. I even called her "my little angel," but at the time, I had no idea how true those words were.

When Lora turned two, I realized that I needed God in my life. I didn't want Lora and my son from a previous marriage to grow up without knowing Jesus. So we found a church to attend, and I started living for God and teaching my children the Bible. I thought I would lead the way, but from the very beginning, Lora ran ahead of me spiritually. She embraced God with all that she was—so determined and on fire for God. She didn't have all of the baggage that I had. With her fiery red hair, she was stubborn—but in a good way—stubborn in her faith for God.

Lora is now thirteen years old, and she is still flourishing in the Lord. She is so full of life, joy, and wisdom. And she is so precious. Last Mother's Day, she wrote this poem for me:

My Mother

I love you and you are the best
You fed me when I was a baby.
You rocked me to sleep.
You taught me the "Word"
And you loved me.
You are my beautiful, wonderful, great mother
That I love and care for very much.
by Lora Frost

I wept as I read her heartfelt words. Even after all of my mistakes. Even after all of the hard times we'd gone through. Even though I hadn't always done everything right. She still loved me—just like Jesus. She is always telling me that I am the best mom in the whole world, at which I say, "Thank you," but think, *You have got to be kidding! Don't you remember this morning when I lost my patience with you?* But amazingly enough, she never remembers my shortcomings; she only remembers my good qualities—just like Jesus.

Learning from Lora

You know, in most families, the children grow up wanting to be like their parents, but I find myself wanting to be like Lora. Her faith is so big and untainted. She loves the Lord and totally believes that what He says He will do, He will do. I have seen her faith at work many times. Sometimes it is for her, but most of the time, she uses her faith for others.

When she was five years old, she wanted a "My Size Angel Barbie." She asked me for it, and of course, my thought was, *I am not spending over $150 on a doll! You have got to be kidding me!* As a single parent, I didn't have the extra money to purchase the doll, so I just told her I would put my faith with hers, and we'd believe together for that "My Size Angel Barbie." I have to admit, I didn't have much faith to put with hers on that particular item. But she never forgot it. For two years, she believed God for that Barbie. Then, one day I was on the Internet just browsing, and God spoke into my spirit and said, *Do a search for that Barbie.*

Yeah, right, I thought, *I don't have that kind of money to spend on a Barbie doll.* But in obedience I searched for that doll, and to my surprise, up popped a Web site selling a "My Size Angel Barbie" for only $50! And again to my surprise, I actually had that much extra money in my account. So, Lora got her "My Size Angel Barbie." She never gave up. I believe God supernaturally lowered that Barbie doll's price so that she could have one.

Her faith and never-give-up attitude taught me much that day. But the lesson had just begun. A few years later, we were watching Christian TV as we got ready for work and school, and Lora became entranced by a program called "Life Today" with James and Betty Robison. This particular broadcast was about feeding children in Africa. James shared a story of a mother and her three children who had walked for two days just to get something to eat.

"Can you believe that, Mom?" Lora asked, visibly upset.

"That's awful, isn't it?" I commented as I packed her lunch for school.

At the end of the program, the announcer shared how much money it would take to feed five children for a year—$82.

"Mom, can you take the money you saved up for my Christmas presents and send it in to the children?" she asked, her big blue eyes staring up at me.

> Even after all of my mistakes. Even after all of the hard times we'd gone through. Even though I hadn't always done everything right. She still loved me just like Jesus...
>
> —Karen Frost Underwood

"Honey, I've already purchased your presents," I told her. "In fact, most of them are already wrapped."

"Well, I'll just have to believe God for the money to send those children," she said matter-of-factly.

Having learned from the Barbie experience, I stopped what I was doing and prayed with her. We prayed that God would help her get the money to support those five children for a year. She only had $3 and some change, but she was determined to get the money for those hungry kids.

When we finished praying, Lora smiled and said, "It's a piece of cake for God."

Then she added, "Oh, and while I am at it, I am going to believe God for money to buy my own Christmas presents for the people on my list."

I smiled, but inside I was worried. I thought to myself, *There's no way she can get that kind of money!*

Well, sometimes we adults just don't get it! That night I sent Lora to bed and a few minutes later I heard loud talking in her room. I hurried down the hallway, intending to turn down the radio when I realized—it wasn't the radio at all. It was Lora praying. I leaned my head against her door and listened. As she prayed, tears began to fill my eyes.

"Father, I thank You that You are our Source," she prayed, "and I thank You that we have food to eat every day, even if it is not stuff I like all the time. Father, in the name of Jesus, I lift up to You that lady I saw on TV today, the one who walked two miles for food. I thank You that she is blessed and her tummy is full, and Father, that she and her kids have 'too much food and too many houses to live in.' And Father, I thank You that I have the money to send in for food for those children and to buy Christmas presents this year. Amen."

I stood in the hallway with tears running down my face, realizing that my daughter's heart was right where it needed to be. Within about two weeks of Lora's prayer, she had almost $100 to send to the children. And a week later, I received an unexpected Christmas bonus and was able to give Lora the money to buy her own Christmas presents! Isn't that just like God?

My little angel is growing up, and so am I. We are growing together in the Lord. Whenever I get discouraged or sad, I just look at Lora. She is truly my inspiration, and I thank God that He gave her to me—even though I didn't want a baby at that time. Every day we're together, Lora tells me, "You're the best mom in the world." While I know that's not true, I do believe that she's the best daughter in the world, and I'm so glad that she's mine.

Karen Frost Underwood works in the publications department for a worldwide ministry. As a fulltime mother of two (plus two stepchildren), Karen still finds time to pursue her love of writing. She also enjoys spending time with friends. She and her husband, James, live in Saginaw, Texas.

The Piano Lesson

Cheri Henderson

A little girl, so precious, on the piano bench beside me,
with tiny fingers, curled just so, she learned to play each key.
And all her songs were beautiful—for how could they not be?
Every time she played a song, she played it just for me.

Then the child became a teen, and the flute became her song;
and when she marched upon the field, I could have listened all night long.
All her songs were beautiful—for how could they not be?
She didn't know it, but each time she played, she played her song for me.

And today, my precious, darling girl, I just wanted you to know
what a blessing it's been to watch you and to see the way you've grown.
And though you may lay the music aside, I'll still have the memory
of each and every beautiful song that you sweetly played for me.

Yes, every time I think of you, it will be with much delight,
and in those times I'll pray for you—God's blessings on your life—
that your love for Jesus grows and grows and never goes away—
and He'll always be your sweet, sweet song through the night
and through the day!

Cheri (Gale) Henderson, a resident of Waynesville, Ohio, acknowledged Jesus Christ as Lord and Savior of her life on April 11, 1983. She began writing "lyrics for the Lord" the week after she dedicated her life to Christ. Her Web site, "Poet of Praise," has provided inspiration and encouragement to thousands of visitors.

Heart to Heart:

Have you ever wondered if you're really capable of being a mother? What situation caused you to doubt yourself?

Have you given those feelings over to God?

What are some lessons that your children have taught you?

Given to God

Esther Numa

Is it possible for a newborn daughter to save the life of her mother? That's what happened in my case. Everything started out so beautifully. Jim had a promising career as a minister, and I had always dreamed of being a minister's wife. I thought we would have the perfect marriage. After all, ministers taught others about faithfulness and purity. We were both young and attractive and totally in love; people commented that we were the perfect couple.

But we were living a lie.

Drifting from God

Everything was wonderful until Jim began to spend a lot of time with some very liberal-thinking ministers. They began to discuss the newly published magazine *Playboy*. In the interest of "morality," they decided that someone should purchase a copy so that they could know firsthand what was being offered to the men in their churches. Jim didn't hesitate to purchase the literature for the group. It all seemed harmless and for a good purpose.

A short time later, the men went to a conference called "The College of Christian Life." They spent very little time in the religious meetings; most of their time was spent in pornographic movie theaters and nightclubs where girls were dancing. Jim didn't try to hide his activities; he actually had convinced himself that it was just the "cool" thing to do. After all, the ministers in his group were doing it.

It became a yearly "guy" thing. Each year when he left for the annual meeting, I became sick inside. I saw his whole attitude deteriorating. Family life seemed less and less important to him. We argued a lot. I was afraid—afraid of losing my home and our life together. I couldn't believe we had sunk to such depths. We believed the Bible, but it no longer played a large part in our lives. It had become just a source book, something as a basis for his weekly message.

He began bringing home porn magazines on a regular basis, and then he started stopping in actual pornography shops. Every time we were out, he stole long looks at other women. I didn't handle any of it in a righteous way. I accused, criticized, cried, and totally aggravated the situation. We were in a downward spiral.

A Light in the Darkness

I began to toy with thoughts of alleviating my mental stress. Each time I opened the medicine cabinet, I stared at the pill bottles and wondered which could be lethal in large doses. I daydreamed that I would be out of my misery and everyone would pity my husband. His life would go on relatively unaffected.

Then, in the midst of all the pain, I found out I was pregnant. Over the months, my swollen body didn't make me feel any better. I felt ugly and compared myself to the pictures in Jim's magazines. I could never measure up. The days seemed to grow darker and darker.

One morning the pains began, and only two hours later, I was holding a shining light. In the midst of my darkness, God had sent an angel to brighten my days. In my desperation I clung to that baby. My life was a wreck. One day at a weak moment I put the baby in her crib and went to the closet where we kept a handgun high on the shelf. I stood on my tiptoes and reached up high, until I felt the cold dark steel in my hand. I pulled it down from its place and held it in both hands, thinking of the decision I had before me.

As I sat there contemplating how to end the pain, I heard a small cry from the crib. I looked into the face of that angel. I began to imagine what her life would be like growing up knowing that her mother had been so weak. Somewhere deep inside, I heard a voice saying, "*I didn't create you for this.*" I fell to my knees and began to cry. I knew that God cared about my situation and had literally spoken to me. Sobs poured from the very depths of me. I felt like I was at the bottom of a deep well, but as I looked up, I could see the light. Repentance poured from my soul to the ears of God. I lifted my baby from her bed and held her tightly.

One Day at a Time

One day at a time, I sought God's help in restoring my life and mental health. I realized that I had to deal with my own attitudes and that only God could change my husband. Little by little, I felt inner healing taking place, and to my surprise, the more I released my husband's problems to God, the more I saw change take place in him. We were becoming a close-knit family again.

Just as we were experiencing the hand of God in our lives, a small church down state requested that we come. I knew it was divine leading. We were finally ready to be the spiritual leaders we had been "called" to be. My daughter continued to be a strength to me, but I knew deep down that that kind of relationship wasn't healthy. I still mentally clung to her.

God, She's Yours

When my daughter was five years old, she caught a cold that wouldn't go away. On Christmas Eve she was terribly ill. Finally, I couldn't stand it any longer and insisted we rush her to the emergency room. She had a high fever, and as I held her in the car, I was terrified that we were losing her. All the way to the hospital, I begged and pleaded with God to allow her to live. Once again I heard the still, small voice: "*Would you still trust Me if your daughter didn't live?*" I wept and clung tightly to the small form in the blanket. As we pulled in the hospital drive, I cried out, "God, she's Yours!"

The doctors swept her from my arms. Nurses ushered us into the waiting room.

It seemed like an eternity before anyone returned to speak to us. A nurse came to relay the doctor's message: "It's possible that she has spinal meningitis." The words sent a chill through me. But I had told God that I would trust Him, no matter what happened. I called my mother, who knows how to pray. Others from our church were praying, too. All night we prayed, sometimes in the chapel, sometimes at her bedside.

All the way to the hospital, I begged and pleaded with God to allow her to live. Once again I heard the still, small voice: *"Would you still trust Me if your daughter didn't live?"* I wept and clung tightly to the small form in the blanket. As we pulled in the hospital drive, I cried out, God, she's Yours!

—Esther Numa

In the wee hours of the morning, the nurse informed us that she was out of danger; she had pneumonia, which they could treat. I began to rejoice and thank God for sparing her life. I again affirmed that I had given up my claim to her; she was not mine, but His.

Over the years, my daughter and I have shared a special bond. She has always seemed to know when I'm hurting or lonely. She calls at just the right moment to cheer me up. I still believe that she was put into my life as a special gift to me. But I still know she's just "on loan." She now travels abroad in diplomatic service and is in danger much of the time. But I have put her in the hands of God. She belongs to Him. I'm just happy that I've been allowed to enjoy her in the time we have had together.

Esther Numa writes for a local newspaper and teaches in a Bible college. She is a musician, a counselor, and an instructor of language arts in the public schools.

She Remembered

Valerie Cantrell

My child and I sang the sunset together for the first time tonight,
Simple songs from our hearts inspired as we viewed God's display of art.
I asked the Lord to use more purple, my child asked for a bit more pink.
Our request barely spoken, the colors burst forth in the sky, painted by a hand unseen.
I asked my child to remember how God painted the sky especially for us that night,
And if in many years to come she finds herself singing the sunset alone—remember.
There she is, Lord, with her child by her side, my child with her child, what a beautiful sight.
They've come to sing the sunset together inspired by what You will do.
They've come to view Your art in the sky, they wait to see what colors You'll choose.
I hear her praying, Lord, she knows I'm by Your side, watching as You prepare to paint
Your sonnet in thesky.
Hear her as she asks You, Lord, to please use some purple and add a bit more pink, to help her and her child as they sing the sunset—
She remembered.

Valerie Cantrell lives in Texas with her husband of twenty-four years and their son and daughter. She considers it a privilege to support her husband in his role as minister of music and associate pastor. She works as a TV/video editor at a ministry and loves her role as mother. Sweet daughter, this is for you.

Up Close and Personal:

Spend a few moments thinking about your children—their strengths, their weaknesses, their callings, their giftings, their uniqueness. Now, jot down three special qualities you have identified for each child. Take a moment and record your thoughts. Then, when the time is right, share your writings with your children. You might even write a poem or create a collage of words and pictures, focusing on your child's beautiful traits. These would make wonderful gifts—presents your children will cherish for a lifetime.

Magnificent Maggie

Patti Iverson

"Maggie! Get down from the top of the refrigerator right now!"

"Now, where is that little imp? Oh? You found her in the baptistery?"

"Please don't kick my baby out of the nursery! She's not even two!"

"But Mrs. Iverson, she's crawling out onto the roof of our third-story building, and we can't handle it!"

Sigh ...

These were all familiar descriptions of Magnificent Maggie. My daughter's pixie blue eyes glittered with delight. Her rosebud mouth was always raised in a special smile as if she communicated with angels. Folks called her Miss Personality and loved watching her, all bouncy and blonde! But Maggie was a handful.

We purchased a special harness to corral her in her bed. Forget the crib. She continually climbed out of that and hurt herself at a wee eight months old. Maggie pushed her twin bed over to the window, shimmied up, and out she went after jimmying the window lock.

My dear friend volunteered to baby-sit while my husband and I went on a much-needed vacation. Who knew she'd scale the armoire, down an entire bottle of iron pills, and need to have her stomach pumped?

Scary trips to the emergency room seemed to be the norm. Six times before she was even one year old.

"Here come the Iversons again!" We usually didn't even have to pay the co-pay because they immediately popped us into a room to take care of the problem at hand. 'Twas a sad day when Maggie stuffed sixteen raisins up her nose. The dear doctor took his long, steely tweezers and began pulling out the swollen fruit that was blocking her breathing. Yuck!

One summer day a knock on the door startled me during my "moving in," muddled madness. A strange man stood there with my tiny fifteen-month-old darlin' daughter, naked as a jaybird, saying, "Is this little one yours? Folks in the house at the corner said she might belong to the new people who just moved into this place. I sell Kirby vacuums. Might you be interested?"

Oh, sheesh! My delight in a fenced backyard evaporated. It wasn't a tall enough fence to corral the happy little wanderer. Drats! Not to mention my embarrassment at the state she was in—or wasn't!

When our little family enjoyed nature camping along the Umpqua River in Oregon, we momentarily lost Maggie. Randy and son, Peter, had gone fishin'. Maggie was in her playpen while I delighted myself in a novel. I only looked away for a few minutes, but the playpen was empty. The entire campground and rangers were all searching far and wide for a little eighteen-month-old babe. Her whiny little voice finally answered Pete's cry.

"Here I am! I went potty all by myself! I'm a good, big girl now!"

She was in the men's outhouse. I can't bring myself to contemplate what would have/could have/should have been… Maggie's guardian angels have done an amazing job guarding her!

It would take a book to write all the escapades of magnificent Maggie, so I'll leave that for a later date and jump into the present. Today she is a beautiful, godly, married young woman. She loves the Lord and plays classical piano as if it's for His ears alone. She's been involved with young, unwed mamas and jailed women who have made big mistakes in life. Her church is blessed as she's on the worship team, uses her gift of hospitality with Bible studies in her home, and serves as the church secretary. As she accompanies musicals and singers on the piano, she reaches out to them with the love of her Lord.

I'm delighted to be part of her heart and life, to share the Yahweh sisterhood with her, and wouldn't have changed one magnificent Maggie moment for anything in the world!

Patti Iverson lives in Medford Oregon, with her fire chief husband. She's a writer, part-time clown and Mrs. Santa Claus, and spiritual leader of a ladies Bible study. She writes calligraphy, reads, and cooks while keeping in touch with her two grown children. God has blessed her with glorious women in her life, and she is thankful!

Celebrate the Moment:

This week, do something fun with your kids. If you have little ones, declare Saturday a "mixed-up day" and wear your PJs all day long; eat pizza for breakfast and pancakes for dinner; and sleep in a tent in the middle of the living room. If you have tweens or teens, let your cool kids pick out your clothes or do your hair—scary! They will love it, and you'll survive it. If your children are already grown and on their own, call them and thank them for all of the magnificent moments you have shared together. Then, plan a time in the near future for a "make-a-new-memory" day or weekend.

Intimate Details:

She's a woman beyond compare. My dove is perfection, pure and innocent as the day she was born, and cradled in joy by her mother. Everyone who came by to see her exclaimed and admired her—All the fathers and mothers, the neighbors and friends, blessed and praised her.

Song of Songs 6:9 MSG

Train a child in the way he should go, and when he is old he will not turn from it.

Proverbs 22:6

Inspirational Insight:

Our children are truly gifts from God—precious treasures from heaven. While we have a moral obligation to teach our children and guide them in the things of God, I am reminded daily that I, too, am still learning. We are growing up together. Sometimes I wear the teacher's hat, and other times, I wear the student's. I am thankful for both fedoras. And I'm thankful that God chose me to be Abby and Allyson's mother. (He must have known I'd need good teachers!)

Maybe you're in the middle of raising your children, and you feel like you're doing everything wrong. Or perhaps you're an empty nester, with regrets—dwelling in the land of "should haves." Or, maybe you were never able to have children of your own, and there's a part of you that hurts every time Mother's Day rolls around.

No matter where you fit, God has an answer to your question and a bandage for your hurting heart. He loves you, and He wants you to know that you don't have to go it alone—not one more day. If you need wisdom to get you through your child's teen years, God's got you covered. If you need reconciliation with a grown child, God will lead the way. If you long for a child in your life, God can fulfill that desire, too, in ways you might never have fathomed. Whatever you're struggling with today—give it to God. While mothers know a lot, remember—Father knows best.

Heart to Heaven:

Thank You, Lord, for my children. As I look into the faces of my children, I am so full of gratitude and love. I praise You for giving me these precious gifts. Father, help me to love and nurture my children the same way that You love and nurture me. Help me to pass on a heritage of faith and family, and give me the wisdom to speak into their lives on a daily basis. I worship You today. Amen.

Chapter Eight

THROUGH THE GOOD, THE BAD, AND THE UGLY:

Friends Who Stick Together through All Kinds of Weather

A friend loves at all times.

Proverbs 17:17

Oprah Winfrey once said, "Lots of people want to ride with you in the limo, but what you want is someone who will take the bus with you when the limo breaks down." Friends who stick around when trouble sets in—those are real treasures. When you're riding high and everything is going your way—everyone wants to be your best friend. But very few friends will ride out a storm with you.

When I was fourteen years old, my entire junior-high cheerleading squad tried out for freshman cheerleader—all five of us—along with 70-plus other girls. We were all vying for six coveted spots. At the end of the day, my best friend Angie had made the squad, and I had not. To make matters worse, we were leaving for spring break right after the list was posted, and I had asked Angie to go with me on vacation.

I wasn't sure how it would go. Would she think she was better than me? Would she want to stay in town with the other freshman cheerleaders?

Not Angie.

She proved she was a friend for life.

We both crouched down in the backseat of my parents' car and cried all the way from Indiana to Florida. By the time we hit Orlando, I had very puffy eyes and a best friend who loved me—no matter what. Today, we are still best friends. We've weathered many storms together—her parents' divorce, my father's long illness and death, her miscarriage, my cross-country move—so many struggles, side by side. I know she's there for me, and she knows I'm there for her—no matter what. It's those "no-matter-what" kind of friends that make our happy moments happier, and our tough times bearable. If I do nothing else on this earth, I hope I can be a "no-matter-what" kind of friend to those who need me. *MMA*

Heart to Heart:

Has there ever been a time in your life when you felt all alone? Meditate on that time for a moment.

What caused this feeling of abandonment and hopelessness—did you shut out your friends? Did you shut out God?

Since then, have you learned to let others in? If so, describe the difference that quality decision has made in your life.

Reach Out and Live

Leigh Platt Rogers

When I transferred to the College of William and Mary in Williamsburg, Virginia, I was very much on my own. As a transfer student, I was not able to find housing on campus and ended up living alone in a small apartment about three miles away. I felt small, lost, alone, and disoriented.

But that was not the real problem that sophomore year. The year before, as a freshman at a "party" school in Florida, I had felt extreme pressure to "fit in" with the tan, thin, beautiful girls all around me. I tried diet after diet to keep my weight down—and I was not fat—but I felt this need to have the perfect body.

After I'd been in Florida for a full semester, struggling with schoolwork and social pressures, I discovered a miraculous way to be able to eat anything I wanted and not gain a pound. Today it is called *bulimia* and is a recognized, worrisome eating disorder.

Eating disorders are strange, mysterious, and insidious. In the beginning, I felt I was completely in control over what I could eat. Unlike the anorexic, who starves herself, I did not become significantly thin. I was eating plenty, so I looked "normal."

Of course, I always had to leave the table after eating to go to the bathroom. Soon the binging and purging cycles started to happen more and more often. Every morning I woke up and promised myself that I would not eat "too much" so I would not feel like I had to purge, but every day I broke that promise.

I found myself caught in a vicious world of abnormality and unreality.

I also found I wasn't the only one caught in this destructive cycle.

First Impressions

I met Jessica* during an initiation into a sorority at William and Mary.

We, as pledges, were told to dress in our initiation outfits. We began to strip off our T-shirts as directed and put on the white gowns. As I dressed, I happened to glance over at Jessica who was next to me and drew in my breath with horror. Shock coursed through my body as I could easily see every single rib bone and the sunken shape of her stomach. She was terribly thin—almost skeletal—and reminded me of the pictures I had seen of prisoners of war.

Instinctively, I knew there was something wrong with her. I also knew that her problem was not very different from my own. That night, after our initiation ceremony, we celebrated and toasted each other with champagne. Having had nothing to eat, the alcohol went straight to my head and loosened my tongue. I put my glass together with Jessica's and leaned forward, whispering in her ear, "There's something wrong with you." Alarmed, she drew back sharply. I saw the fear in her eyes.

"I know," I continued, "because there is something wrong with me, too."

She stared at me; her hollow face and tortured eyes spoke of her pain. Silently, she moved away and avoided me.

The next time I saw Jessica was about two weeks later. I ran into her while walking to class. As soon as she saw me, she tried to avoid eye contact. She probably would have passed by if I had not said, "Hey, Jessica. I'm sorry I scared you."

I took a deep breath because it looked like she was going to ignore me, but to my relief, she looked directly at me and stopped. Her shoulders slumped, and suddenly she looked exhausted.

"It's okay," she said.

"Look, I spoke the truth, but I was not trying to scare you or make you mad," I shared. "I saw you at the initiation. I know you have a problem, but I have one, too. You're not alone."

Suddenly, she opened up and blurted out that she was on her way to see a therapist. Her mother was threatening to take her out of school if she did not gain some weight. I told Jessica I thought I should be in therapy, too, because I was also fighting a horrible problem with food. I told her I was scared all the time. I saw relief in her face and gratefulness for my honesty in her eyes.

By the end of the semester, we had become good friends. I moved onto campus, into a dorm across from Jessica's, for the second semester. We slowly got to know each other better. It is interesting, however, that the eating disorder—which controlled our lives—was a subject we avoided. It was "taboo" until one memorable day.

Valleys and Shadows

It was a gorgeous, sunny spring day. After my morning classes, I raced back to my dorm to don my swimsuit and begin working on my tan. I headed to a favorite grassy spot between our two dorms and laid out my blanket. I sighed with happiness as I felt the warmth of the sun.

Perfect.

A few minutes later I felt a shadow. Jessica stood there in her jogging shorts and T-shirt, covered in sweat. I shaded my eyes to see her better and started to say hi, but before the word could leave my lips, she fell to her knees. She was in a complete and utter panic. Her eyes were full with tears, and her mouth trembled.

I grabbed her hands, which were ice-cold, and said, "Jessica! What is it?"

She swayed back and forth, shaking her head. She could not speak. I was getting scared.

"Jessica! What is wrong?" I shook her hands, raising my voice as panic gripped me. "What? What is wrong? *Tell me*!"

She tore her hands from mine and covered her face. Between heaving sobs she uttered, "I want to die."

"What?" I asked, stunned.

She pulled her hands from her face and I saw an agony so great that my heart hurt for her. I felt my own tears begin to well up as I heard her say, "I just want to die. I'm going to kill myself. I can't take it anymore."

My mind reeled. I had no idea what to say. What do you say to someone who is in such pain? I, too, was afraid. Afraid of saying the wrong thing. Afraid that she really meant it.

I knew why she wanted to die—I had experienced my own inner desperation and despair.

I opened my mouth and said the first thing that came to mind: "Well, you just can't."

She looked at me blankly. It was probably not what she expected to hear.

"Jessica, you can't die," I urged. "I need you. You're all I have."

I took her in my arms and hugged her tight. I said over and over, "You're my only friend. You can't leave me here alone. We have each other. We can help each other. We can get better."

She cried in my arms like a tired, scared, exhausted child.

That moment marked a turning point for both of us. I did not realize how close I had come to losing my friend until she told me later that she'd had her suicide planned for weeks. She had a razor ready. She knew what to write in her note. When she finished her usual morning jog, she had planned to go to her room and take a bath with the razor.

It wasn't until she returned from her jog that her resolve crumbled and she felt something drawing her to the other side of the dorm where I was sunbathing.

When she saw me, she hesitated, but a strong force moved her forward. She hadn't planned to talk to me—but thank God, she did.

To this day, I thank the Lord for His help. Had it not been for a sunny day; had I not decided to sunbathe; and had Jessica not seen me, I might have lost her. Somehow she found the strength to reach out for her life. Together, we were able to help each other through difficult times.

We each sought additional help through therapy. The closer we became, the more I helped her see that life was worth living—and she gave me the strength to acknowledge that I did not have to be perfect. Today, thanks to the Lord, we continue to have a loving and close friendship that I would not give up for anything.

"If you (or someone you know) are struggling with an eating disorder, go to www.eatingdisorders.com for listings of treatment centers and other useful information."

*Name has been changed to protect her privacy. "Reach Out and Live" is an excerpt from *Nudges from God*, an anthology of inspiration, compiled by Vanessa K. Mullins, published by Obadiah Press.

Leigh Platt Rogers was raised all over the world by virtue of her father's occupation (CIA). A graduate of the College of William and Mary, Leigh currently resides in Benicia, California. She has been published in *Spies Wives, Nudges from God,* and *Sticky Situations: Stories of Childhood Adventures Abroad* .

Up Close and Personal:

Is there someone in your life who has been there for you—no matter what? How about you? Are you the kind of friend who weathers the storms of life beside your buddies, or do you take shelter elsewhere? Take a moment and record a few of the times your friend has supported you. Now, write the times you've supported her.

Welcome Home

Dena J. Dyer

"Welcome Home, Carey and Dena!" the note on our front door read. "What's this?" I asked, and he just grinned.

As we stepped into our tiny apartment, my mouth hung open. The place sparkled—not an ounce of clutter or dust anywhere.

It was 1:30 a.m. As first-year seminary students, Carey and I had spent an entire week and several weekends working at our day jobs and then wolfing down fast food in the car while driving to rehearsals for a Christian theater production.

Ironically, this week was called "hell week" by the cast, since we were only a few days from the show's opening. The 150-member cast and crew spent evenings from 7 to 11 p.m. (or later) going over our movements, fitting costumes, and practicing our scenes.

Each day, we guzzled caffeine at our day jobs and told ourselves it would only last a few more nights. Exhausted yet exhilarated, Carey and I assured each other we'd clean our house and car later … after we were back in the land of the living.

Dropping my bag, I walked through the living/dining/kitchen area and noticed that the dishes were done—by hand, since we didn't have a dishwasher. The living-room floor had been vacuumed, and the linoleum in the crackerbox kitchen had been swept and mopped.

"Who did this?" I asked Carey. He shrugged and laughed.

I made my way into the bedroom, where the bed had been made. A note taped to the pillow read: "Enjoy, you lovebirds!"

"It was Andrea and Lee, wasn't it?" I asked. "She must have borrowed the key from you."

Carey nodded. "She asked me for it yesterday, but she wouldn't tell me what she was up to—only that they and the Hartigs were planning a surprise."

Lee and Andrea Chitwood and Jason and Sharon Hartig, our best friends, were two young married seminary couples from our church.

Though they had all been happy for us when Carey and I were cast in *The Promise*, they were somewhat disappointed when they found out we'd be tied up on weekends for six months.

"This is incredible!" I exclaimed. "Our friends are so thoughtful."

Carey yawned. "Yes, it was," he agreed, limping toward the bed. He was in his pajamas, with his head on the pillow, before I could blink.

"We'll thank them in the morning," I said.

I knew the Chitwoods and Hartigs probably wouldn't appreciate a 2 a.m. wakeup call—even from two extremely grateful friends.

George Eliot once said, "What do we live for if it is not to make life less difficult for each other?" and I agree. During that extremely busy season of life, my best friends taught me that simple acts of kindness (often unasked for, and many times undeserved) are the sweetest gifts of all.

Dena Dyer is a wife, mom, writer and speaker from Texas. She loves to encourage women to find their hope, rest and joy in Jesus—our only true source of peace in the midst of a chaotic world. Her books include *Grace for the Race: Meditations for Busy Moms, The Groovy Chicks' Roadtrip to Peace* and *The Groovy Chicks' Roadtrip to Love.*

Sisters in All Seasons

Susan Lugli

Lying in my hospital bed, I cried. As I waited for my friends to arrive to spend their Thursday night with me, I remembered all of the times we had shared over the past twenty-five years. Our family had moved ten years prior, but our sisterhood stayed faithful.

A horrendous accident had turned my life upside down. My husband, Rusty; my adult daughter, Nikki; and I had been in a motor-home accident: We were all badly injured and severely burned. Since that fateful night, my friends had been driving four hours roundtrip every Thursday after work to be with me. This incident was the worst any of us had shared together.

As I waited for them to arrive, my thoughts drifted back to our early twenties when we met in Woman's Bible Study Fellowship. We were all young wives and mothers trying to grow in our faith, and through time, our relationships grew, too. We experienced many life difficulties together, such as children problems, separations from our husbands, drug addiction, failing parents, and many other issues.

My friends became family to me. We were always there for each other. Even though there had been separation by distance, we still planned special times together each year. We made a pact with ourselves to never lose touch—even if we only made a phone call each week. We had too much history together, and that could never be taken from us and never replaced.

Challenging Times, Faithful Friends

During this most challenging time in my life, I knew I could trust and depend on my sisters in the Lord. At the beginning of our incident, there was nothing anyone could do but wait. Both my husband and I were on a live-or-die list. He stayed on the list for the first two months, and I was taken off after a week. From that point on, my friends took a silent oath that they would not stop coming to be with me until they knew I would be okay.

It was a very difficult time for everyone involved—even my visitors.

Some got sick to their stomachs when they entered the room, and others actually fainted, but not these friends. They put on the gown, gloves, and masks in case of infection. They ignored the smell of burned skin and medications. They didn't seem to mind that the room was hot with no fresh air to breathe, nor that I looked like a monster all wrapped with white gauze. I lay there, unable to do a single task for myself. My back was broken, and I had to lay totally flat and not move, but I could smile. They made sure I did.

I remember the first time my friends took me downstairs in a wheelchair to a burn support-group meeting. All four of us were afraid of what we would see and hear. They asked a lot of questions. All I could do was cry. We were living in a world that none of us understood.

After my release from the hospital—two long months later—those same friends continued to visit each Thursday for six months. They were there for me when I learned to take my first steps of recovery. They were my prayer warriors, my comforters, and my counselors. I depended on them and shared each aching moment of pain and concern with them. I remember the night we shared before I saw my husband for the first time following the accident. I had refused to see him until I knew he was going to live. I did not want to have the memory of him hooked up and burned. We had been together since I was fifteen, and I wanted to remember the good times. It had been ten weeks since the incident, and I was much stronger and able to feed myself and take a few steps. He had awakened out of his coma, and I was told that he would live.

Our son had gone to the hospital to take Polaroid pictures of him to show me when my friends arrived. Each one sat beside me in a circle and we passed the pictures around. I can't express the fear I felt as I looked down at them. The room was silent except for the sobs.

It was a sad season in all of our lives, but we shared it together. There were many people who took part in our full recovery. My neighborhood rallied around to help in many ways, and my local Bible study girls took turns feeding, walking, rubbing, and exercising me. They all walked the journey with us and have been able to share in our success story and happy ending.

The Lord said in Romans 8:28 that all things will come together for good to those who love the Lord and are serving His purpose. Watching the sacrifice of many friends and the power of prayer has healed my family.

Susan Lugli is a Christian speaker and author. In 1998 she wrote "Out of the Fire," an article that was published in *Today's Christian Woman*. That same year, she was profiled in the *Women of Faith New Testament Bible*. Susan is now living on a family ranch in Lompoc, California.

Ordinary Person, Extraordinary Impact

Sharon Norris Elliott

A Christian song I heard more than twenty years ago said, "God uses ordinary people…who will give their all, no matter how small their all may seem to you."

I know someone like that. She is an ordinary person who has made an extraordinary impact on my life. She is not the product of famous parents; has no debilitating physical challenges to overcome; and hasn't yet accomplished some outstanding achievement that has caught media attention. Mary Flett, my friend, simply keeps the love of her Savior in view as she lives out her faith in tangible ways that bless others.

Mary's gentle caring for me as a friend came sharply into focus when the foundations of my marriage began to crumble. The deeper my problems got—financial ruin, physical and emotional abuse, the loss of my home—the closer Mary stood by me. Without my even realizing it, I started to experience depression. One day during faculty devotions at the school where we both work, Mary named me as someone whose faith she admired. I was stunned because it seemed as if I couldn't possibly be an encouragement to anyone else as I struggled daily just to keep my own head above water. Still Mary shared, "I admire Sharon's faith because she has kept her hope in the Lord and her testimony before her students, even in the midst of all the troubles I know she's facing."

That comment was just the beginning of how Mary has lifted me over the years. When I finally made the agonizing decision to separate from my husband, it was Mary who welcomed my boys and me into her home until I found an apartment. It was Mary who stealthily returned with me to my condo to retrieve my computer, television, and clothes. It was Mary who worried about me but stuck by my side as I went through an unhealthy, rebound relationship. She even loaned me money several times and has patiently waited to be paid back as God has slowly lifted me out of my financial valley. And it was Mary who took us in once again while my new house was in escrow, so I could save a month's rent to put toward the down payment.

The impact Mary has had on my life has grown out of her unfailing readiness to extend herself to me. I have learned compassion from her because she refused to see me as any less of a person, woman, or Christian, just because life was "happening" to me. Whether through an encouraging word or sharing her living space, she has shown me how to bless another person's life by using whatever God has given me at the moment. As the song lyric says, her little has become much in my life.

It's a lifestyle thing with Mary, and I'm thankful to God for using her to show His hands and His heart to me.

Sharon Norris Elliott is an author and popular speaker whose messages touch the hearts of her audiences at conferences, retreats, and other functions. She also teaches high school English and journalism at a Christian school in Inglewood, California, near where she, her husband, James, and their two teenage sons live.

The Gift of Peace

Carol Fox

I met "Anna" at a time in my life when I really needed a friend. I have never been very good at making or keeping friends. Though I've been repeatedly told this belief is groundless, I always feel self-conscious and inadequate where other people are concerned.

Anna, I'd been told, was "really super…just a *great* lady." That statement alone made me want to meet her—and scared the pants off me at the same time. Come to find out, there was no reason to worry. Everything I had been told about her was true, and then some.

God had put us together; I knew it at once. Though close in age, we're at very different stages in our lives. She had married and started her family early, while I waited, and waited, to make those commitments. She has children in their late teens to early twenties, while mine are still six and not quite two. Still, our journeys have been remarkably similar, and as much as I love her as a friend, Anna has also been a teacher, counselor, sister, and role model for me.

It seems that no matter what I'm going through, Anna has been through a variation of the same situation. She blesses me with the wisdom she has gained from the various trials God has brought her through. There are so many ways I want to be like her: her strength, her ease with people, her wisdom, quick wit, and easy laugh.

There was one way, however, I was always glad we were different. And I hoped we always would be.

Love through Loss

Anna had confided in me that several years before we met, she had suffered a miscarriage. And *suffered* was an accurate word. She had been devastated physically, as well as mentally and emotionally. And while she had recovered mentally and emotionally, she still had lingering physical problems stemming from that traumatic event.

This was the one area I had always been glad we differed. I couldn't imagine the anguish of losing a child, no matter how brief that life had been with me.

I told myself that I was a strong Christian. I said all the right things. I tithed. I went to a faith-filled church. I'd had a great pregnancy and delivery with my five-year-old son. In fact, I even worked for a worldwide ministry!

One Monday I discovered that I was five weeks pregnant with our second child. My husband and I didn't hesitate to tell everyone. I mean, I'd had absolutely no problems with my first pregnancy. Friends, family, and coworkers were all thrilled for us.

Because I looked forward to another uneventful pregnancy, it never occurred to me to be concerned when I started spotting that Friday morning. At my husband's insistence, I called my OB who told me to come in immediately for tests.

Unfortunately, timing was against us. I didn't arrive at the doctor's office until late Friday afternoon, and the test results wouldn't be ready until sometime Monday. My doctor ordered me to bed and told me to call if I had any more symptoms over the weekend.

Though my symptoms increased, my faith remained strong. I knew everything would be fine. I just *couldn't* have a miscarriage. I kept telling myself over and over that when I called on Monday the tests would prove me right. I felt so strongly about it that I even went back to work Monday morning.

When the nurse called to say I had indeed miscarried, I was stunned. Feeling totally lost, I didn't know what to do. I called my husband at work and delivered the horrible news. He was devastated, as well—even more so since he couldn't come home and comfort me. He urged me to call Anna.

Anna. I knew Anna was involved with her own family that day and I didn't want to intrude. But I had nowhere else to turn, and I knew I couldn't be alone.

I called, and my God-given friend dropped everything to welcome me into her home and give me all the comfort and wisdom I so greatly needed.

She told me about the peace with which God had enveloped her after the loss of their child. She said she believed that there is peace, and then there is the Gift of Peace—that supernatural peace God drops on those who otherwise might not make it through some loss or trial in their lives. The trial still remains, but somehow you are wrapped in an infinite, impenetrable peace.

It was still hard. It was hard to not think of what my child in heaven would have looked like when he was my son's age. Would his arms have felt the same when I got my nightly hug? It was hard when others told me that if my faith had been stronger I would have been able to carry my baby to term, implying that some weakness in me was to blame for this tragedy in our lives.

But not Anna. My sweet friend held me while I cried and prayed for God to grant me the Gift of Peace as He had done for her those years before. And as faithful as God is, He did.

She stood by me through a very difficult next pregnancy, when I was placed on bedrest many times and felt so scared I would do something wrong and lose this baby, too. She encouraged me, made me soup, and best of all, made me laugh. She came to the hospital when my daughter, Shelby, arrived five weeks early, and reminded us of God's love and faithfulness as our tiny infant spent a week in intensive care.

Anna is the godmother of my children and the gift God has placed in my life forever. We have shopped together, cooked together, laughed together, and wept together. We have traded stories, jokes, recipes, and clothes. I cannot think of a more giving, faithful, joyous, loving friend. And the best part is, she says the same thing about me.

Carol Fox lives in Fort Worth, Texas. She is a freelance editor, and a wife and mother of two. In her spare time, she enjoys decorating, cooking, and shopping.

Celebrate the Moment:

Think of someone who is going through a difficult time and do something for her. Take her to lunch or send her a balloon bouquet—anything to let her know you're supporting her.

Intimate Details:

Do not be anxious about anything, but in everything, by prayer and petition, with thanksgiving, present your requests to God. And the peace of God, which transcends all understanding, will guard your hearts and your minds in Christ Jesus.

Philippians 4:6–7

Inspirational Insight:

Let's face it. Life can be really difficult. While it's comforting to know that God promises to never leave us nor forsake us, sometimes we just need a tangible hug. That's what friends are for—to hug the hurt away.

Maybe you've been on the receiving end of those hugs lately. You may be going through a nasty divorce, battling an extended illness, or facing a different battle in your life, and God has placed some wonderful friends by your side to help you make it through. Or, maybe you've been the giver of hugs, showing God's love to a friend in need.

No matter which end of the hug you happen to be on at this time in your life, God wants you to know that He loves you even more than your best friend in the whole world. He will heal your hurting heart, and He will help you reach out to those who are hurting. If you are in need of a "no-matter-what" kind of friend today, ask God to bring one into your life. And then look for opportunities to be that kind of friend to the people in your world.

Heart to Heaven:

Lord, I thank You for putting friends in my life—especially during those times when I need them most. Lord, I know that You have handpicked my friends, and I am so grateful. I see You shining through them. Father, I ask that You help me to return the love that I've been shown. Help me to be the kind of friend people can count on—no matter what. Help me to be more like You—for You are the ultimate Friend, the ever-faithful Friend, the Friend who sticks closer than a brother. I love You, Lord, and I praise You for being my best Friend. Amen.

Chapter Nine

WORDS OF WISDOM:

Timeless Advice from Wonderful Women

If you accept my words
and store up my commands within you,
turning your ear to wisdom
and applying your heart to understanding,
and if you call out for insight
and cry aloud for understanding,
and if you look for it as for silver
and search for it as for hidden treasure,
then you will understand the fear of the LORD
and find the knowledge of God.
For the LORD *gives wisdom,*
and from his mouth come knowledge and understanding.

Proverbs 2:1–6

Wisdom. It's something we all need. Ask any mother of a two-year-old child or newlywed bride and she'll tell you that knowing how to think and act is a moment-by-moment process. And if she's a Christian, she's praying for God's wisdom every step of the way.

There's value in knowing how to live. There's value in wisdom.

Whether through God's Word, through our own experiences, or by the lives and words of those around us, we have to seek wisdom out. The difficult wisdom that we gain from divorce or death is bitter. But if we pause a moment, we also remember the joyful wisdom that comes from birth and friendship.

As we live and gain wisdom, we have to remember that we're a part of His master plan. As we receive His wisdom, the time will eventually come when we get to pass it on to others. Others poured their lives into us, and in turn, we're able to exhibit His love and goodness to those around us. Sometimes the effort can merely brighten someone's day, but other times, it can change their lives. *GM*

Heart to Heart:

What piece of wisdom did you gain from someone in your life, either through her actions or words?

Describe the person who gave you that wisdom.

What impacted you the most about what she said/did—then and now?

The Stray that Stayed

Hope Smith

Have you ever noticed that just when you think you have something mastered and all figured out, something or someone comes along and knocks you off your "all-knowing pedestal"? This happened to me about three years ago. (Now, mind you, I get knocked off this well-worn seat on a regular basis.) However, I thought (emphasis on *thought*) I had this "love-your-neighbor" thing figured out. Sure, I was kind to those who were kind to me and even asked how my "neighbor's" family was doing. You know, chitchat. But the conversation never went much deeper than the surface level. That is until Mrs. Rippy came into my life.

That spring day I thought I would take advantage of the nice weather and clean out the car. My children had buried a stashed treasure of candy wrappers and unwanted Happy Meal toys that they ever so cleverly hid in the crevice of the back seat. As I diligently went about my task, I heard a voice calling to me. Not one of my children's voices, and not the still, small voice of the Lord, but one I had never heard before. One of age yet resonating with authority. When I emerged from the safety of the back seat, I noticed the elderly mistress of the house across the street waving her arms, motioning me to come near. For some reason, it was like I was back in my childhood; I began to think of anything wrong I might have done. Nothing came to mind. (I'm no angel, I know, but I could think of nothing that would concern this stranger.) In confusion and fear of the unknown, I obeyed the call.

"My knees are bad, and I'm afraid I'll fall down these old steps. My name's Ruth, Ruth Rippy. What's yours, dear?"

Since I was taught to respect my elders, I answered quickly, "Hope." Opening the door and walking in, she said for me to come in and visit a spell. So I did.

As we talked, I still wasn't sure why exactly she had summoned me. But I did notice one thing. Cats. Everywhere you looked there were cats. Cats of painted glass and ceramic on tables, hanging on the walls, pictures and clocks imitating the feline form. On the couch, a woven throw bearing a repeat of this favored companion with the stuffed version resting atop the soft folds. Everywhere. Of course, I asked her *the* stupid question: "So, do you like cats?" I wasn't being sarcastic, I promise. The query popped out of my mouth before I realized it. She did, but as it turned out, everyone seemed to give her cats in the form of a gift. She made mention that she had kept the real thing for as long as she could take care of them; now her old age limited her. However, that didn't keep the strays from coming around to lie on her porch. So, in a way she was still able to enjoy their company.

Upon my leaving, I noticed that my hands were clenching the tops of two full garbage bags. As it was trash day, I offered to take them out to the curb. This one act would lead me on an adventure to discover the wonderful mystery of this intriguing lady.

It became a ritual—every Tuesday morning found us sitting and talking about her life gone by. I had told myself that I would feel horrible if something had happened to her while she was alone. Her children lived out of town, and it was only the occasional visitor who saw her. I knew I would want someone to check up on my elderly mother if I were in her kids' shoes.

Sure, that's what I told myself. The truth was that I enjoyed talking to her. She may have been over fifty years older than me, but we were kindred spirits. She was independent and spoke her mind. A bit of a rebel. It was funny, for someone who never got out or dated after her husband, Charlie, died, she had more boyfriends than you could shake a stick at. Every business in town knew her. The local pharmacy that brought her prescription; the delivery boy was her boyfriend. The plumber; her boyfriend. The mailman; her boyfriend. The owner of the hardware store; her boyfriend. You see where this was going? They weren't her boyfriends in the traditional sense; but they all did things for her. She had a way to charm, just to ask, for the things she needed. And these people seemed to enjoy being in on her joke.

Which brings me to Charlie. He was the true love of her life and the topic of most of our conversations. He had died years before right after a physical to become a state trooper.

"The doctors didn't know what they were doing. One had given him a pill without the other one knowing about it. He died that night in his hotel room right after he called to tell me and the boys goodnight."

I was told about him on a regular basis, as if for the first time. Her aged mind forgot all the many times before. It was all right with me, though; it appeared that she was trying to reconnect with the memory of him each time the story was told. Then she would turn to me with a look of sadness in her eyes and say that she didn't know why the good Lord was still keeping her alive. She wasn't any good to anybody down here. I'd protest and tell her that God must have some reason and that *I* needed her. I *did* need her! I needed her to show me how to care for someone other than my own family members. In doing so, she became that to me. God used her in that way. I also needed a friend. Not that I was lacking in that area—I have many friends. My best friend and I have known each other for the majority of our lives. However, Mrs. Rippy needed me. She needed others to help provide her everyday necessities. She had a "boyfriend," Bill, who bought her groceries. Another old friend cleaned her house and made sure that her lawn didn't become overgrown. And me? She needed me to sit and talk a while (and I needed to know that she wouldn't hurt herself carrying out the trash).

Watching her interact with all these people, her "angels" she called them, showed me something I had missed in my pursuit to know it all. Her relationships mirrored the one Jesus wishes to have with each of us. Although she was alone, not lonesome, she was content and full of joy. Yet, she knew when and how to make her requests known. Sometimes it was just to have a silly conversation. God brought her into my life at just the right time. Being recently divorced, I was of the mindset that I had to be self-sufficient. I must do it all for myself and not ask for help. Let me tell you, this is a very dreary path. In my giving to her, I also received a gift—a priceless gift: true friendship. God kept her here until the full measure of that lesson was learned.

I can look out my kitchen window, and now, like always, the stray cats warm themselves and rest easily on the porch across the way. As for this stray, God has shown me what it means to love your neighbor, literally. And through knowing her, I have found where I belong.

Hope Smith is a single Christian mom, freelance writer, and interior designer living in Sulphur Springs, Texas, with her three children: Kaitlyn, Timothy, and Johnathan. She writes on the restoration and design that God has for each person's soul. Hope also writes on being a Christian single today.

Out of the Mouth of Babes

Laurie Barker Copeland

I have a special friend who keeps me on the straight and narrow. I love this friend dearly because she challenges me to be the best I can be and loves me unconditionally. However, it's just plain hard to take good advice from a twelve-year-old. Yes, this all-knowing, Confucius-like friend is my fashion-conscious, eyeball-rolling daughter, Kailey. I always say the reason God put children on this planet was to keep their parents humble.

The saying "out of the mouth of babes" didn't spring from a black hole. I'm sure it came from a parent after an episode similar to this: After many years of dreaming about visiting Glacier National Forest, the day had finally arrived. We had planned on camping, and had heard that the Many Glacier Campground had the best views and sold out quickly. Nonetheless, we decided to try and secure a campsite at Many Glacier on the opposite end of the park, before it sold out. After racing over mountain and stream, we arrived at Many Glacier with only three campsites remaining. We quickly snatched one up. When I wondered out loud what that cute little building, located right smack in front of us on our campsite, was. My husband informed me that it was the RV "*dump* station."

I had *really* looked forward to a getting-back-to-God-and-nature vacation, but this "dump station" was something else. I hate to admit it got to me...bad. I sulked around, grumbling, "I can't believe we're finally in this beautiful park, and all we can see is this *dump* station!"

But then Kailey crawled up in my lap, and said, "Mommy, look! You can *still* see the mountains from here!" As I sat there, still pouting, a spiritual lesson was formed in my head. How many other times had I let the small, inconsequential "dump station"-like problems get in the way of my view of God's master plan?

Such circumstances can look huge, blocking out God's plan. But if I looked beyond the dump-station stuff, I can see the purple mountains' majesty.

Those simple words from an eight-year-old set my eyes on what was important: the view *beyond* the ugly stuff right in front of my face.

> How many other times had I let the small, inconsequential "dump station"-like problems get in the way of my view of God's master plan?
>
> —Laurie Barker Copeland

The very next day, we secured the best campsite in the park, overlooking not only the majestic mountain, but also a clear stream that we set our tent right next to. The soft sounds of the river reminded me all night long of how God used the sweet voice of an eight-year-old to show me how to not let "dump stations" stand in the way of true beauty—and God's big picture.

Laurie Barker Copeland is a speaker, humorist, actress and shower singer. She is co-author of *The Groovy Chicks Road Trip to Peace* and *The Groovy Chicks' Road Trip to Love*, and is a contributor for *Caution: Children Praying; Humor for the Teacher's Heart; But Lord, I Was Happy Shallow; Your Spiritual Personality* and other books. She holds Girlfriend Getaway women's retreats and her latest adventure is playing the part of "Pepper" with The Groovy Chicks at women's conferences. Her favorite production performs daily at her Orlando home with her husband, John, and daughter, Kailey, who are constant sources of material for Laurie's stories.

If You're Young Enough

Cheryl Browder Speir

My birthday was not a huge milestone, but it definitely put me in the over-forty-five bracket. Since my family was taking me out to celebrate, I decided to treat myself to a shopping trip at my favorite salvage store. Digging through the overstuffed racks looking for bargains is a favorite pastime of mine. Maybe I could find a nice dress to wear.

And there, hanging on a rack was a wonderful dress full of tropical colors. It was long and flowing; I loved it. This was the dress for the night's festivities. Then, out of nowhere, the thought came: *You're too old for that dress. Only women much younger than you should wear such vivid colors.* Sadly, I agreed, placed it back on the rack, and continued looking. Now my heart wasn't in it, and for the first time in my life, I felt old.

From that point on, everything I picked up seem to scream, "You're not a young woman anymore! Quit trying to dress like one and go find the granny dresses!"

Lord, I silently prayed, *I always thought that with Your help I would be prepared for whatever came in my life. You have been so faithful to make me ready for every stage of life. I really don't mind getting older, but I sure don't like the idea of drab, matronly clothing. You're going to have to help me resolve this issue.*

Just then, two ladies walked in the front door of the store and immediately caught my eye. They appeared to be in their late seventies and were completely dressed up as if going to a social. One wore a navy pantsuit and the other was dressed in a pastel blue dress with a straw hat that sported a rose. Their hair was freshly done, and their makeup was flawless. I felt quite mousy next to them.

Listening to them talking, it was obvious that they had been friends for many years. They laughed and reminisced about raising their children, and they spoke of their late husbands, swapped recipes, and kidded each other about silly things they had done in the past.

As they moved about the store, I found myself following them, staying an aisle or two away so I could listen in on their happy chatter. They were just what I needed to fight the sudden onset of the blues.

They found bargains for themselves, and constantly kept a look out for things the other would like or look good in. The things they picked out showed how exactly opposite their tastes were, yet they respected each other's style and knew them well. One liked romantic pastels with lace and ruffles. The other was drawn to conservative, business-type suits.

What a friendship, I thought. *They have weathered the storms of life together. That's the way I see my best friend and me being if we could only spend more time together.*

Feeling self-conscious about following them around, I decided to leave before they thought they were being stalked. Gathering my items together, I began to walk toward the cashier to pay for them. That's when I heard it, the best advice I ever received, and the answer to my prayer.

"Oh, look at this blouse!" the one wearing the hat exclaimed with delight. "With all those colors, I could wear it with anything."

She was more excited over this find than she had been over all her previous ones.

"Do you think it's too young for me?" she asked, with doubt creeping into her voice.

"If you're young enough to like it," her friend said with firm conviction, "you're young enough to wear it!"

I stopped in my tracks.

If you're young enough to like it, you're young enough to wear it.

What wisdom, what insight! Her friend tossed the blouse in her buggy. I walked over to the dress aisle hoping that the colorful dress was still there. It was. That night I looked great in the dress I was young enough to wear.

Cheryl Browder Speir is married to her high-school sweetheart and lives in Southern Mississippi. Her hobbies are gardening, writing, and crafting. She writes a recipe column for LePicayune and is the editor of Write 2 the Heart, an e-zine of inspirational and heartwarming stories.

Up Close and Personal:

If you could share one bit of Christ-like wisdom with someone you love, what would it be?

How did you learn this?

Who shared it with you?

The Book of Friendship

S. A. "Shae" Cooke

December 24 fell with heavy snow that clung stubbornly to the roads. Highways closed and the authorities issued travel advisories. Still it fell, sealing in the somberness of the day.

Let it snow, I thought. It was my first Christmas Eve without my mother and the sadness of that thought battered the day's excitement. Any excuse not to leave the shelter of my small apartment was good.

The telephone rang. I ignored it and went to my bedroom to bury my face in the softness of my pillow, hoping to muffle out the incessant and demanding shrill. It was eight-o'clock and I was supposed to be at my friend Rebecca's house for dinner.

"I'm doing her a favor by not being there," I murmured. "How can I be joyful when I feel so lousy? I just want to be left alone." My eyes fluttered with the weight of the tears that would not stop. My heart felt as heavy as the falling snow; my grief piled high.

How do I stop missing my mother?

I must have drifted off to sleep, for I awoke with a start. Someone pounded at the front door. I tiptoed to the window and looked through the frosted pane. Seeing Rebecca's car parked out front, I padded back to bed and drew the covers over my head.

"Girlfriend," she shouted. "I know you're in there! Answer the door!"

"Leave me alone!" I shouted back.

The floorboards creaked in the hallway. I heard paper rustling as she slid something under the door.

"Merry Christmas," she called out.

Not answering the door made me feel worse, if that was possible. I wasn't being fair to my best friend. Since grade school, we had been inseparable. Most people mistook us for sisters, even though we looked completely different. Her hair was long, thick, and sunset red in color, and I sported a short, blonde bob. Her father and sister had died in a car accident when she was eight years old. As a result, her mother had to return to work, and Rebecca was pretty much left to fend for herself. We had always been there for each other, but this time, I didn't want her or anyone else near me. My misery kept me from answering the door.

> Over the following months, my storms took refuge within the pages of the book. Tears fell onto the paper as often as words. Prayers were tearfully written, and faith was renewed.
>
> —S.A. "Shae" Cooke

When I was sure she had left, I retrieved the small, square package. Wrapped simply in gold foil, it had no other decoration. Carrying it to the bench by the window, I sat down and unwrapped it. Inside were a gold pen and a blank journal. When I opened the front cover, a bookmark fell out, and on it a note:

Dear Friend:

My words won't heal the pain. However, your own words can.

Love, Rebecca

I stared at the blank pages, not wanting to spoil the pure whiteness with empty phrases. A single tear fell, and the page absorbed it. I wrote my name on the first page and looked at it for a long time.

Out of the corner of my eye, I caught some movement on the windowsill outside. A cat sat crouched, waiting to pounce on a sparrow that had just landed in search of some seed I had sprinkled there earlier in the day. Every time the cat pounced, the sparrow flew away, returning only moments later to eat the rest of the seed. I am a terrible artist; however, to my bewilderment, I sketched several pictures of the young bird as it flew away and returned. Next, I drew the cat, poised and ready to attack its prey. When the cat finally gave up on the sparrow and darted to another ledge, I surveyed my drawings.

Am I the sparrow or the cat? I wondered. I wrote the question beside the drawings and then closed the journal.

Over the following months, my storms took refuge within the pages of the book. Tears fell onto the paper as often as words. Prayers were tearfully written, and faith was renewed. The storm ebbed as each image and word touched the pages.

I was the sparrow, foraging for answers, oblivious to the threat of being swallowed by grief.

As my heart healed, so did my understanding of the incredible friendship Rebecca and I shared. This journal was, in essence, an extension of her friendship. Even though I had pushed her away at a difficult time, she found a way to help me communicate my grief by giving me this "surrogate" friend.

One night, I picked up the phone and dialed her number. She answered on the second ring.

"Looks like the snow is melting," I said. Spring was just around the corner.

S. A. "Shae" Cooke, a Christian freelance writer and mother, lives in Coquitlam, British Columbia.

The Puzzles in Our Lives

Carol Fox

There are times in the lives of all believers when something happens that makes us question God. *Why did this happen? How could this possibly have happened to me/him/her/them? God, why didn't You intervene so that this tragedy wouldn't have occurred?"*

My family went through such a trauma at one time and we, like all Christians, had questions we couldn't answer. I was at a point where I needed answers from a flesh-and-blood person, not just from the pages of my ever-faithful Bible. So, I went to see my pastor's wife.

I had counseled with Lisa on some other issues in the past, so I knew what she believed and I trusted that she would tell me the truth, and that her counsel would be biblically sound.

Still, I entered her office with some trepidation. I don't think we are ever comfortable letting others know we are at a place of doubting God. But Lisa had seen a lot—and been through more—in her many years of serving God. I don't think there was much that could faze her anymore.

When I told Lisa the situation we were trying to come to grips with, she prayed for me and encouraged me, and then she asked me a rather unusual question.

"Do you like to do puzzles?" she asked.

"Well, yes," I hesitantly replied.

Where was this going, exactly?

"Good," she said. "What's the first thing you do when you sit down to assemble a puzzle?"

"First, you put your edge pieces together so you have a framework to start with," I guessed.

I hadn't put a puzzle together in many years. The last one I remember doing was at my grandmother's one Thanksgiving.

"That's right. Then what do you do next?" she queried.

"Then you separate your colors into groups. You know, all your blue pieces together, all your yellow together, and so on" I replied.

The technique was coming back to me, but I still had no idea where Lisa was headed.

"Exactly. Now I want you to consider this traumatic situation your family is currently going through to be a black piece. And I want you to set it aside for now and go work on your yellow pieces and your red pieces."

I was astonished—how could I not focus on this tragedy that was so easily all-consuming?

"And sometime down the road—it may be five months or it may be fifty years from now—you will look back and see that this piece has a place in the whole puzzle of your life."

Wait a minute! Was I just supposed to pretend like this thing *had never happened? I was beginning to doubt Lisa's wisdom after all. But then she said the words that have kept me on course and validated all the emotions involved, while still allowing me a way out of my grief.*

"Now don't get me wrong. This will *always* be a black piece. Time will never turn it red or yellow or blue. But, if you set it aside for now and focus on the other important things in your life, one day you will look back and see that this is just a piece in the whole picture of your life."

They say time heals all wounds. While I don't necessarily agree, I do believe time gives perspective. We all have black pieces in the puzzles of our lives. But with the perspective of time and distance from the pain, if we really look, we can see that those black pieces don't engulf our picture. And perhaps we can recognize that those dark places may actually give definition and vibrancy to the reds and yellows and blues that make up the pictures of our lives.

Carol Fox lives in Fort Worth, Texas. She is a freelance editor, and a wife and mother of two. In her spare time, she enjoys decorating, cooking, and shopping.

Celebrate the Moment:

Take time to call or write someone who has inspired you with her wisdom. It doesn't have to be a long or drawn out explanation—just take a moment to brighten her day and let her know you're thinking of her.

More Than a Meal

Mel Ann Coley

Sometimes I have experienced God's love in unexpected forms.

For me, it came in the shape of my grandmother's homemade biscuits!

As a child I always felt Granny's love when my family visited her Texas farm.

And the next day would begin with a noisy rooster and the smell of fresh, hot biscuits.

Each meal my grandmother prepared was a true Southern feast.

So sometimes I watched her cook and saw the love in her preparations.

My family gathered at the table and filled themselves with good foods from the earth.

But it was more than just a meal; our conversations and laughter also fed my hungry soul.

Mel Ann Coley is a published author, teacher, and freelance writer. Currently she is a part-time writing teacher at Richland College in Dallas, Texas. Her publications include a variety of educational materials, poetry in the *Every Woman* newsletter, and a children's play, *The Day Miss Grouchy Melted.*

Her Name Is Ruth

Jessie Innmon

Her name is Ruth, how appropriate as she gleans among the fields;
Not for wheat and barley but for daisies and daffodils.
She has an eye for beauty that God provides for us;
So many never notice and she shares it with a plus.
I come to work each morning to a beautiful bouquet;
Of such varied colors, arranged in a wildflower spray.
She uses her gifts to the fullest, never missing the opportunity;
To use them to reach the lonely, so Jesus they may see.
She's such a busy lady spreading beauty around the town;
She makes her moments count toward her eternal crown.

Jessie Innmon was a church secretary and a single mother of a teenager when she wrote this gratitude poem to Ruth Johnson in 1990. She now lives in Austin, Texas, and is a grandmother of five. She serves currently as prayer chairman for Woodlawn Baptist Church and is part of their ministry to the homebound.

Intimate Details:

My mouth shall speak of wisdom; and the meditation of my heart shall be of understanding.

Psalm 49:3 KJV

She openeth her mouth with wisdom; and in her tongue is the law of kindness.

Proverbs 31:26 KJV

Inspirational Insight:

God uses the people in our lives, even those who only briefly pass through it, to sharpen and teach us. Then in time, we hopefully have the opportunity to brush bits of wisdom on to someone else. We get the distinction of sharing the love of Jesus, of making the lives of the people around us—even our acquaintances—a little better.

If we take a moment, we can probably remember someone who gave us her wisdom: a mother, a daughter, a neighbor, a pastor's wife, a friend. Perhaps it was a mother, who, like mine, gave some sage advice, such as, "Never think you're better than anyone else." Or a grandmother who, again like mine, gave the seemingly simple marriage advice, "Always keep a sense of humor." (Only later did I realize how profound her advice was.) It may have even been someone you knew long ago and lost contact with, but it was the person God chose to use at that moment because He loves you. He knew exactly what you needed.

Maybe you've faced a tragedy, and right now, it takes all your effort just to make it through the day. You need His wisdom. If so, take a moment to ask God who you can trust. Sometimes the people you're drawn to in a crisis aren't the ones you see every day.

And if you're the one God chooses to use to share some wisdom you've received, consider it a privilege! Out of everyone He could call—tag, you're it! You'll have the opportunity to show His grace and goodness, and bring peace to a difficult situation.

Heart to Heaven:

Lord, thank You for calling me to be a part of Your family and for making Your wisdom available to me. I acknowledge that I need it every day. And as You give Your wisdom to me, help me to share it with others. Help me to take time to share Your love and kindness with everyone I meet through my words and my actions. I pray that everything I do be pleasing to You and bring those around me closer to You. Amen.

Chapter Ten

FRIENDS REMEMBERED:

Tributes to Someone Special

There is a time for everything… a time to weep and a time to laugh, a time to mourn and a time to dance.

Ecclesiastes 3:1, 4

There is also a time to remember.

Many people come in and out of our lives, but very few leave a lasting impression. Those whom we remember become a part of us. Even after they're gone, they stay with us—in our hearts. They live on in our memories.

That's what this chapter is about—remembering those friends who have made distinct engravings upon our hearts.

As a former reporter for a daily newspaper, I have been privileged to meet many interesting people. I have interviewed celebrities like actor Nick Nolte, college basketball coach Bob Knight, and singer Bob Carlisle. I have spent time with senators and governors. But of all the people I encountered as a reporter, Jane made the greatest impact on my life.

The last time I saw Jane, she was covered in chicken pox for the third time that fall due to her weakened immune system, but yet she was still talking of God's goodness. I was amazed. I looked at this Christian mother who had lost her husband to a terrible disease—the same disease she was fighting—and I wondered how she could have such a love that seemed to radiate all around her.

After several visits to her home to interview her, she became more than just the subject of a newspaper story. She became my friend. I deeply regret that I didn't become her friend sooner. I wish I'd had more time to know her. I wish I could have told her how much her friendship meant to me. I wish I could have made her pain go away. I wish so many things when I think about her.

I still miss Jane, and I am thankful for everything that she spoke into my life. That's why I want to honor her with this—her story. *MMA*

A Legacy of Love: One Woman's Story

Michelle Medlock Adams

Porcelain and wooden eagles adorn Jane's southern Indiana home. In the living room hangs a painting of an eagle with the words "They shall mount up with wings like eagles" written below the majestic bird.

Her husband, John, always liked eagles. He even had an eagle tattooed on his arm while he was in the marines. After he became a Christian, he wanted to have that verse added beneath it.

"He just never had a chance to get it done," Jane said. "He was kind of embarrassed that he had a tattoo. He thought maybe people would take him the wrong way. I think he regretted getting it done."

John regretted a lot of things from his younger, wilder days.

Before he met Jane, he lived life on the edge. But in 1985 all of that changed. He and Jane began dating and soon fell in love. They got married, pledging to love each other "until death do us part."

Shortly after the wedding day, Jane became pregnant. Nine months later, they welcomed a baby girl to the family, giving Jane's five-year-old son from a previous marriage a little sister. They were a family.

"I'd never been happier in my whole life," Jane reflected.

The Nightmare Began

John and Jane (not their real names) decided to build a new home that year. John was a skilled builder, so he took on the project by himself, but a couple of months into it, he became ill.

John went to a local doctor and was diagnosed with pneumonia. After ten days on a strong antibiotic, his condition hadn't improved. His physician told him that he had contracted the flu on top of pneumonia and prescribed some additional medication. Still, John's condition worsened.

A week later he was admitted into a local hospital, where doctors ran test after test—including an AIDS test—trying to figure out why John wasn't responding to the medication. To his horror, the AIDS test result came back positive. The nightmare had begun. Immediately, John was transferred to an Indianapolis hospital for further testing. There, the results were the same—John had full-blown AIDS.

After some serious soul-searching, he concluded that he'd contracted the disease from a previous heterosexual relationship before he had become a Christian.

"I couldn't believe it," Jane said. "I just kept thinking, *This can't be happening! Not to us!*"

John's doctors told Jane that she needed to be tested, too.

"I was scared," she admitted. "I didn't want to know."

But she knew she had to find out for her children's sake. If she had the disease, it was likely her daughter would also be infected.

Jane bravely took the AIDS test—she would know the results soon enough.

The waiting only increased her inner battles. Worry, anxiety, and anger flooded her soul as she thought about what was happening. In the midst of her difficulty, she sought the strength she needed from the Lord. She needed to be strong for her husband—for her children. She couldn't allow herself to be angry at John, not now, not when he needed her the most. She made a conscious decision that day—*I won't dwell in the "what ifs" and "should've beens," because it will destroy us.* She decided to live day to day, clinging to the promises of God that her grandfather had taught her at an early age.

When the test results came back, Jane, her father, and her sister headed to the facility to learn the news. When they reached the office, they were led into a private room and asked to sit down. The man with the results looked at Jane and said very solemnly, "Your test shows you're HIV positive."

Jane felt as if someone had kicked her in the stomach.

"I couldn't even breathe," she remembered.

The man gently took her hand and said, "This does not mean you are going to die. Don't give up."

Jane's dad and sister spent the next half hour asking many questions, seeking as much information about the disease as possible. Jane sat very quietly, thinking about her children. Now they would have to be tested, as well.

"I was worried sick about my kids," she shared. "Waiting for my daughter's test to come back was horrible. I wasn't so worried about my son because he was from a previous marriage, but our daughter was ours together."

After only a few days, the children's tests were in.

They were both negative.

"That was the first bit of good news we'd had in weeks," Jane recalled.

She sent word to John about the children's test results. For days he had worried about his daughter. He was sure she would test positive.

"She's a miracle if you really think about it, because I gave birth to her," Jane said. "God was looking out for us, or else she would have AIDS. John called her 'his little angel' because she is such a miracle."

Treasured Moments

After seven weeks on life support, John's body began to fight back. He recovered enough to leave the hospital. When he came home, he began attending church and reading his Bible.

"He turned his life totally over to the Lord," Jane said.

She was already drawing her strength from God each day. She had grown up in church. Her grandfather was a minister, so she knew where to turn.

"I couldn't have made it without the Lord," she said. "And my family and friends have given me a lot of support, too."

Jane and John accepted their fate and praised the Lord in spite of it all. They spent time reading the Word together and praying with each other. Those were special times, but there were difficult times, too.

"You get used to being sick," Jane said, pointing to several bottles of pills prescribed to her. "The hardest time I can think of was when we told the kids that Daddy was dying."

> Jane left a legacy of love. She made the most out of the moments she had here on earth. The waves of her love continue to wash over the world through her family and friends. Her story will forever be in my heart, encouraging me to live every minute for God and take advantage of every opportunity to love those important to me. I can think of no better way to honor her memory and her precious friendship.
>
> —Michelle Medlock Adams

The doctors advised the couple to tell the children. Their little girl wasn't old enough to understand, but their son needed to know. The doctors told them he would need time to emotionally prepare for the inevitable loss that was coming.

Shortly after John came home from the hospital, the couple took their ten-year-old son into the living room, and John said, "Honey, you know how you've been seeing all the news about Ryan White and how sick he got?"

The little boy nodded his head and said, "It ain't fair that he died."

"No, it isn't fair. You're right," John continued. "Well, Daddy is sick, too, just like Ryan White."

The boy buried his head in John's chest and cried for a long time. Then the family pulled together and vowed to enjoy the time they had remaining.

Ready to Go

John died in the fall of 1993—six days before his thirty-fourth birthday and one month after Jane was diagnosed with full-blown AIDS.

"He was ready to go," Jane said, her voice cracking. "He wasn't bitter. Before he died he told me, 'Honey, Satan can do anything he wants, but he can't take away my salvation.'"

He also gave her one last instruction: "He told me, 'Don't ever, ever, ever give up on the Lord.' I didn't intend to."

The song "I Want Us to Be Together in Heaven" was played at John's funeral.

And today—they are.

Jane died in 1996, leaving her parents to raise her children. AIDS may have taken her life, but it never broke her indomitable spirit. She didn't die angry or bitter or regretful. To the very end, Jane was thankful to her God. She continued to love until her spirit left her.

The last thing she said to me was this: "I'm not afraid to die. I'll just be crossing over. You know, I've been blessed. I know my life doesn't look that good right now, but it will someday—when I get to heaven."

Jane left a legacy of love. She made the most out of the moments she had here on earth. The waves of her love continue to wash over the world through her family and friends. Her story will forever be in my heart, encouraging me to live every minute for God and take advantage of every opportunity to love those important to me. I can think of no better way to honor her memory and her precious friendship.

Michelle Medlock Adams holds a journalism degree from Indiana University and a passion for writing in her heart. An award-winning journalist, she has received top honors from the Associated Press and the Society of Professional Journalists. She is the author of 22 books, including *Little Blessings From a Big God* and *Daily Wisdom for Working Women.* She is also a popular speaker at women's conferences and writers' conferences around the country. She is married to her high school sweetheart, Jeff, and they have two daughters and three miniature dachshunds.

Heart to Heart:

Have you ever lost someone very close to you?

How did you get through that time?

Are you still dealing with immense feelings of loss and grief?

Do you have a friend who is currently going through the grieving process?

Are you the kind of friend she needs right now?

Garlic Grace

Sharon Hinck

"What you really need to do is eat more garlic," said one of the women in the church narthex. She tugged the hem of her crisp brown blazer and frowned at me over the top of her glasses. "It cures everything."

I shrugged deeper into my rumpled sweater. Bulky clothes helped hide the bones that showed as my body battled an illness that had resisted diagnosis or help. I was wasting away. I had given birth to my fourth child a few months earlier, and in the secret dark moments of the night, I wondered if I'd make it to her first birthday.

When I became sick, the church's young moms did what they do so well. They brought soup, sent cards, helped with carpools for my older children, and took care of my two-year-old. Their warmth and love kept me going through the misery of illness and medical procedures that were sometimes worse than the sickness itself. But as time went on, the tone began to change.

"I sell a vitamin supplement that is exactly what you need. If you had been on this before, you wouldn't be so sick now," said one man who stopped by our house with a fistful of pamphlets.

"Which doctors have you gone to? You should really go to Dr. Cuthbert. He helped my sister when no one else could figure out what was wrong," said one woman making her weekly call to find out why I wasn't better yet.

"Since God hasn't healed you yet, there's got to be something He's trying to teach you. If you would just figure it out, He'd let you get well," came the twisted theology—sometimes as directly as that, sometimes more subtly.

I understood their frustration. I'd been on the prayer chain past the respectable length of time and still wasn't better. I was a walking billboard for the inexplicable and confusing events that can hit a placid Christian life.

A Call for Help

Depression crept in quickly, and I had no emotional resilience to deal with all the well-intentioned advice that accompanied the cards and soup. So I called the church and asked for help. Our church had volunteer lay-counselors to support people in times of grief, illness, or other struggles.

Susan (not her real name) was assigned to visit me on a Wednesday morning. On Tuesday, I suffered complications from a medical procedure. I was up all night, and by morning told my husband, Ted, something was very wrong. He bundled me up and sped to the emergency room. By the time we arrived, I was fading in and out of consciousness. I wasn't aware of much around me except the horribly bright lights of the ER. At one point I heard soft voices. I wondered who Ted was talking with and turned my head to look. Susan stood with him.

A few days later, we were able to have our first official meeting. She perched on the edge of my bed with a glossy bag full of tissue-wrapped gifts: pajamas, a journal, and some lemon hard-candies to take the edge off my nausea.

"When your mom told me Ted had taken you to the hospital," Susan said, "I decided to head over there." She tucked a strand of her dark hair back into her loose bun. I tried to apologize for not having someone call her, but she just laughed. "It was kind of exciting."

"How did you get in?" I asked.

"I just asked for you at the ER desk and said I was from your church. They assumed I was your pastor, so they let me in."

Susan patted my hand, and there was mischief in her grin. The picture of this PTA mom conning her way past the ER desk made me giggle. She joined in. Soon we were laughing so hard, we were hugging our stomachs, tears running down our faces. Then she gave me a big hug and asked how she could help.

I admitted my frustration with all the suggestions I had received from friends and church members, like the advice to eat more garlic.

Her brows came down.

"You know better, right?" she asked, crossing her arms. "You are doing the best you can. They have no clue what is going on. I know they mean well, but it's just plain silly."

She paused a moment. "Would you like to pray?"

"I would."

We did.

The next week, I met her at the door when she arrived and she handed me another gift. Her eyes sparkled as I pulled it out of the bag. It was an industrial-size jar of minced garlic. About five hundred servings. I laughed so hard I slid down to the kitchen floor. She joined me there, and we laughed away all the silly comments that had loomed so large in my mind.

She visited faithfully every week for a year. Slowly, medical help and time began to improve my health. Though left with some chronic health struggles, I began to adjust to a "new normal." The formal relationship between Susan and I ended, freeing her to meet with a mom in our congregation whose child was battling cancer. Our family moved across town shortly after, and joined a new church, so though I cherished her friendship, it drifted to occasional phone calls, a few gatherings of friends, and Christmas letters.

Walking the Road Together

Then her family joined our church. Delighted to get a chance to see her on a regular basis again, I called and left her a phone message to invite her to join our small-group Bible study. She didn't call back. That Sunday I saw her after church and gave her a quick hug. Her thick dark hair was pulled back in her usual soft bun, and she wore one of her typical country-appliquéd denim dresses. She gave me the same gentle smile she always did, but her eyes looked down too quickly.

"Sharon, could you stay a few minutes? I need to talk to you."

"Sure," I said. I knew she had recently been diagnosed with diabetes. I wondered if she was still struggling with that.

"The reason I didn't call you back is that we had kind of a strange week," she said. "You know I haven't been feeling great? I kept going to different doctors and they all told me something different." She looked up at me and smiled. "You know what that's like."

"I sure do," I said.

"Well, this week we found out why I haven't been feeling good." She took my hands and spoke in the calm way I always heard her speak to her children. "They got some test results back yesterday that show I have cancer in my pancreas…They think I have about six months to live."

She squeezed my hands harder and met my eyes.

"I'll pray for God to heal me. But whatever happens, I want this whole thing to glorify Him," she continued. "That's what I want you to pray for the most, okay?"

I froze. This was a bad dream.

"This is so unfair," I said at last. "You've helped so many other people. You shouldn't have to go through this."

"Don't you see? What we shared helped prepare me. It was a privilege for me to walk that road with you. And I learned so much that I'm going to need in the next few months. Someone already told me I need to go on a diet of nothing but carrot juice and I'll be fine."

We tried to laugh together, but I felt too hollow.

The next several months, Susan was cocooned in the love of family and close friends. When she felt up to it, a group of us gathered at her home each week for prayer. I watched God's grace in action, as Susan's life brought glory to Him through every step of her dark, painful road. I was determined to pray her back to health. She had been there for me when I was sick, and I got better. So, I would be there for her and she would get better.

Instead, the disease took hold. She became too weak for visits. Hospice staff and family pulled in tighter, and I watched from a distance, wishing I could do more. Shortly before Christmas, Susan's husband sent out an e-mail to all of us who had been praying. It was a beautiful testament of his faith as he shared how Susan and her family had prayed together one last time, and then she had gone to be with her Lord.

I wasn't surprised by the heavy feelings of grief and loss. What I didn't expect was how much guilt I felt. I had survived. She hadn't. She had done so much for me, and I had been only able to do so little for her.

> I watched God s grace in action, as Susan's life did bring glory to Him through every step of her dark, painful road. I was determined to pray her back to health. She had been there for me when I was sick, and I got better. So I would be there for her and she would get better.
>
> —Sharon Hinck

But Susan left me one last gift. At her funeral, Lori, one of her best friends from out of state came over to hug me. She had visited Susan during the last days of her life.

"Sharon, I wanted to tell you how much you helped Susan," she said, tears in her eyes.

"What?" I was confused.

"She told me you were one friend who understood some of the things she was going through." I shook my head, but Lori continued. "She told me about the jar of garlic you brought her. She said every time she looked at it, it made her laugh." Lori's forehead wrinkled, "I didn't quite get it, but she said it meant the world to her."

I started to laugh, tears dripping onto my sweater.

"Thank you so much for telling me," I said when I could catch my breath. "You have no idea how much I needed to hear that."

I can't wait to see Susan again in heaven. We'll compare notes about the mysterious tools God used to show us His love during our lives on earth. And I'll thank her again for letting God pour out His grace to me through a jar of garlic—and through her laughter and love.

Sharon Hinck is a wife and mother of four, with an MA in communications. Her articles have been published in *The Upper Room, Christian Parenting, Partnership*, and other periodicals. She is working on a fantasy novel about a woman seeking to follow God's call during adventures in an alternate world.

Up Close and Personal:

Sometimes it helps to put your emotions down on paper. If you're feeling sad today, journal those feelings. If you're missing someone you've lost, write about a special time you spent with that person. Share your heart, and let the healing begin.

Goodbye for Now

Cheri Henderson

I must say good-bye for now; the Lord has called you home.
And though my heart is filled with grief, it's eased because I know
the place that you have gone to is much better than this place.
You've finally met our Savior; now your days are filled with praise.

You'll never hurt or cry again. You've been joined with family,
And I can almost hear you singing as you stand before the King!
Though I know I can't be with you now, this good-bye is not forever.
My friend, I'll see you later, and we'll praise the Lord together!

Cheri (Gale) Henderson, a resident of Waynesville, Ohio, acknowledged Jesus Christ as Lord and Savior of her life on April 11, 1983. She began writing "lyrics for the Lord" the week after she dedicated her life to Christ, and is now a published writer in Billy Graham's *Decision* magazine and many other Christian magazines around the world.

Sweet Refuge

Barbie Jenkins

I was only fifteen, yet I had already experienced so much—so much heartache, addiction, and living on the brink of becoming another statistic of divorce. But thankfully, my parents took another stab at trying to pick up the pieces of our fragmented family and start all over again.

My dad wanted to find a church where, hopefully, our tattered family could find refuge, strength, and healing through the love of God and His people. After visiting several churches, Dad announced he'd found a place for us. Only I accompanied my dad that first night. As we pulled into the dusty gravel parking lot of the quaint country church with its tiny cross-shaped windows on the front doors, it felt homey and pleasant. Even the pinkish glow of the lighted neon cross on the steeple seemed warm and inviting.

Once inside, we were greeted with a couple of friendly handshakes, then my dad's friend swiftly escorted me from person to person where brief introductions and common courtesies were given. That's when I met her. Her voluptuous presence filled a large portion of the end of the second pew from the front. Her once-blonde hair was mostly gray and thin. She was plainly clad in a simple floral duster wearing large white canvas tennis shoes with matching white bobbie socks. Before anyone could say a word, she had taken hold of my hand and enveloped it with both of her large but gentle hands and began tenderly patting mine, as if I were a long lost friend.

Contrary to her size, her voice was delicate and sweet. She introduced herself as Deloris Baker. With bubbly giggles and spurts of laughter, she told me about her children and grandchildren to see if I knew any of them. She further informed me that the little man tuning the guitars was her husband, Harry. With humble pride, Deloris told of her husband's many musical talents, saying he was capable of making music using almost anything.

I found out that night that Deloris could also make music. When she got up to sing before the congregation, she said she wanted to dedicate this song to her new friend, the little "Barbie doll" on the third pew. I was shocked and honored.

"This song is my testimony," she shared, looking directly at me. "It's called 'Thank You, Lord.'"

The words seemed to come from her very heart and her voice sounded like that of an angel. The old bluegrass-type song was about thanking God for simple blessings such as a roof up above, food on the table, and shoes for the feet—things many teenagers take for granted. As we left the church that night, everyone kindly invited us back, but Deloris hugged me and said, "Come back, honey. Jesus is waiting for you, and I think this is where you belong."

I had never met anyone like her before in all of my fifteen years. I liked her. It wasn't long until the little church and its friendly people became our home church. As for Deloris, she continued to tenderly hold my hand for the twenty-two-year journey that followed. She became my trusted and constant friend.

Our age difference didn't matter.

As I watched her everyday life, I learned many lessons—especially humility. Deloris and her husband had very little in worldly goods, but she was always giving—sometimes until it hurt. I can't recall the number of times she phoned from her tiny run-down farmhouse, void of indoor plumbing and with a limited flow of electricity, just to tell me of someone who had a need, someone whom she wanted to help. And it never failed that in the midst of those conversations, she talked about how good God was to her. I realized, even with her large stature, her heart could not be contained.

Together we rejoiced over life's joys. She and her husband, Harry, were there when each of my three daughters were born. I was there when Deloris sang in front of nearly 300 people for a special fundraising event. We weathered life's storms together. Her prayer vigils, songs, and simple words of encouragement carried me. She comforted me when I miscarried; I comforted her when Harry passed away.

During Deloris's last days on earth, I tried to make daily visits to see her in the hospital as she bravely fought the diabetes that had plagued her for far too long. Her eyes had grown dim, her kidneys had ceased to function, and her body was weak and wracked with pain, but her spirit was still strong.

After she had spent several days in the hospital, I knew her time on this earth was coming to a close. Early one morning, before going to work, I quietly slipped into her sterile hospital room and silently prayed over her as she slept fitfully. While standing there listening to her shallow breathing and the whirring and beeping of the machines all around, her eyes suddenly flitted open and she gave a weak smile. Although the words didn't come out, I read her lips when she said, "Hi, Doll Baby." I told her not to try to talk.

She softly patted my hand. In my mind was a blur of precious memories. She kept trying to stay awake and talk to me. I didn't want her to wear herself out, so in desperation, I asked her if she would like for me to sing her a song.

She gave a slight nod. Suddenly the gravity of the situation hit me as I realized what I had just said I would do. My heart was wildly thumping and I thought, *I just can't do this!* But *her* song kept running through my head. Inside my mind I could hear her singing. With a large lump in my throat and a cracked voice, I began the song that truly depicted Deloris.

She closed her eyes and listened; her breathing became relaxed. When I finished the song, I looked up to find that a small crowd of family and friends had gathered at her door and the nurses at the station were watching. For what would be the last time, she touched my hand and breathlessly lipped the words, "That was beautiful." I gave her a kiss and said good-bye. That same hour Deloris slipped into a coma. The next morning she got to see the One who had given her so many blessings for which she was thankful.

Me, I'm thankful for all of my many blessings, but especially for my special friend named Deloris. She continues to touch my life in a way no one else ever could.

Barbie Jenkins loves her family and writing and living for the Lord. Married for twenty-two years and the mother of three teenage daughters, she is a consumer-affairs columnist and staff writer for the *Times-Mail* newspaper, in Bedford, Indiana. She is also the author of *The Legend Of The Christmas Kiss.*

Celebrate the Moment:

Do something special in honor of a loved one you've lost. Plant a tree in remembrance of a friend. Or make a monetary donation to a charity in her memory. Or just spend a few moments remembering the good times you shared with your friend who has passed on, and thank God that you were able to know her here on earth.

Barbara The Artist

Caryl Jones

The artist smiles.
She welcomes me into her peaceful place.
Speaking kindly, she continues with her painting.
Somehow I trust and relax to watch her work.
Such gentle strokes, yet firm and sure,
Add depth and perspective to the beauty of her scene.
Then I see her paints ...
the palate smeared and caked,
mixed from long ago,
I wonder how her picture is so clear.

The artist laughs.
Sometime back, she accepted the challenge,
Deciding that if she were to paint,
She must begin with what she had.
So carefully, prayerfully she examined her colors,
Choosing those which she would use, mourning the loss of others.
Then, like a miracle, I see her
turn the mixed-up paints
into fresh and lively creative scenes;
Reflecting life in hues of love and tints of joy.

The artist waits.
I want to paint like she does.
It seems so natural and free and right.
She takes time to watch my first attempt.
Nothing more than a smear of undefined color.
I hesitate.
But artist that she is, she sees beyond the blur
to what it will become,
and adding that shade of understanding,
I, too, catch a glimpse of what might be.

The artist gives.
Not bits and pieces of her work
As is ordinarily done.
No, much more.
She gives the gift of art itself.
That each who come to watch her paint
May learn to apply their own colors,
recovering the past in new perspective,
painting scenes of healing.
And thus, the artist creates beauty all the more.

Caryl Jones is a registered nurse, a writer, and a survivor. Her poem was written for her friend, Barbara, as a birthday gift some years ago. Barbara suddenly died two years ago, but this poem stands as a tribute to a person who truly let Jesus' love shine through her.

Intimate Details:

He will wipe every tear from their eyes. There will be no more death or mourning or crying or pain, for the old order of things has passed away.

Revelation 21:4

He heals the brokenhearted and binds up their wounds.

Psalm 147:3

Inspirational Insight:

The Bible says there is a time to mourn, but as Christians, we don't have to mourn like the rest of the world. We don't have to feel hopeless and desperate in our grieving. No, we can rejoice because we know we will someday see our family and friends on the other side. We can celebrate the lives of those Yahweh sisters who have already crossed over. And we can make the most of our remaining days here on earth, sharing God's unconditional love with everyone we encounter.

Heart to Heaven:

Lord, I am hurting right now. I miss my friend. I know she is in heaven with You, but sometimes I'd like to have her back here on earth. I am asking You to heal my hurting heart. Please fill my heart with Your love, pushing out all of the grief and sorrow. And, Lord, help me reach out to others who are grieving. Let Your love and comfort flow through me. I love You, God. Amen.

Chapter Eleven

SISTERS OF FAITH:

Mentors, Prayer Partners, and Bible Study Buddies

Charm is deceptive, and beauty is fleeting; but a woman who fears the Lord is to be praised.

Proverbs 31:30

"I prayed, and I believe I'm supposed to go with you," my dear friend Glenda announced.

Astounded, I gaped at her. "Are you serious?"

"Yeah, I've already talked to my husband about it, so just let me know how much the plane tickets will cost," she responded without hesitation.

Her sacrifice was humbling. She paid her way and took precious time off work.

My grandmother had passed away the previous September and her home across country, in Montana, had to be cleaned out. Still missing my grandmother and unsure of what to expect, I dreaded the trip.

Not only was it time-consuming and expensive, it was exhausting. Over one week's time, my mother, Glenda, and I unpacked, organized, and repacked a home that looked like it hadn't been touched in years. In addition to finding my grandmother's belongings, we discovered my grandfather's possessions (he'd died twenty years prior) still in the closets and my great-grandmother's things (she'd died thirty years prior) crammed in the basement.

It was a massive undertaking, but Glenda worked tirelessly from dawn to dusk, as though it were her own family's.

I can never repay her.

Not only did she pray and help during that time, but she made the whole thing fun. We laughed as we scrounged for packing boxes in the supermarket bins and helped keep the well-meaning but inquisitive matrons of that small community apprised of our progress. (Trust me, there was more than one nose pressed against a window.)

She reinforced to me that of all the friends to have, those who share my faith are the best. Why? Because they understand that although I, nor they, have all the answers, we know the Source who does.

A true sister in Christ is more than ready to get on her knees for us, to make us laugh through difficulty, and yes, even go across country to help us do what must be done. And in turn, hopefully, we can do the same for her. *GM*

Heart to Heart:

Describe one of your sisters in faith.

Which of her qualities do you admire?

How has she helped you? Through encouragement? Prayer? Support?

God Collects our Tears

Nancy R. Baker

You keep track of all my sorrows. You have collected all my tears in your bottle. You have recorded each one in your book.

Psalm 56:8 NLT

It's 9 o'clock on Monday evening. I've just completed my list and am seated in my prayer chair next to the telephone. I know it will ring momentarily. Biting my lower lip, I glance over the list and wonder if I've forgotten anyone. Oh, of course, I must add Mack. His eyes have gotten worse.

Flipping through my journal, I smile at the many prayers it represents, mostly requests, but there is a generous sprinkling of thanksgivings, too. Some names appear only once; others emerge week after week. Our Lord did say to be persistent. Sometimes we pray for those we don't know, a chance encounter in the grocery store or someone whose need we have heard about. Often we pray for those who are near and dear to us.

My journal is messy. It has notes and arrows, underlined words and exclamation points—and tearstains. Lucy and I are both criers, and it delighted us to find the verse in Scripture that says God collects our tears in a bottle (Psalm 56:8).

The Faith Builder

This record of prayer is a great faith builder with so many answered prayers. It also illustrates God's sense of humor, like the time I complained about not having enough time to pray. Lucy reminded me that the Bible depicts Jesus as getting up early in the morning to pray.

"Let's ask God to get you up earlier."

I groaned. I am not a morning person. I don't get up easy. Reluctantly, I agreed, thinking it would take an explosion to make me an early riser. For some strange reason, I awoke the next morning at 3:30 a.m. *No, no, no,* I thought. *This is way too early!* I then rolled over and went back to sleep. At 5:00 a.m., my outside cat meowed at the door until I let him in. I immediately dove back into bed. At 5:30 a.m., the recalcitrant cat sat on my chest, licking my nose. Laughing, I reached for my Bible. *All right! All right!*

Ring! Ring!

"Hi, gal, how's it going?"

"Hey, Nancy. It's been a good week. Been busy at work, but that's nothing new. How about you?"

"A little sad. Emilie, my friend with cancer, died Thursday."

"Oh, I'm sorry. We must pray for her family."

A comfortable pattern has formed over time. We first catch up on each other's lives, then we check on the status of prayers from last week, and finally we formulate the list for this week. I pray first, asking for God's presence; Lucy closes in Jesus' name. Then one of us will declare, "Do you have any Kleenex?" and the other will respond, "No, of course not!" You would think after all this time, we would have a box handy, but we really don't plan to cry. It just seems to happen with our heartfelt prayers.

In the Beginning

We are unlikely prayer partners. I am Catholic, and Lucy belongs to the Assembly of God church. Although some of the practices of our churches differ (Lucy wishes for some Catholic reverence in her church, and I wish for some Assembly of God enthusiasm in mine), our foundation is the same—Jesus Christ. We believe that because He is the basis of our relationship, we have remained friends and prayer partners for more than thirty years.

We met when we worked for the same company. We discovered that we both had attended the same marriage encounter retreat and began to share our experiences. Early on, we realized that prayer was a centerpiece for each of our lives.

I was having trouble with my teenage son. He was running with the wrong crowd, and I had discovered marijuana in his room.

"Pray for him, Lucy."

"I will," she responded without hesitation. Then she paused, placed her hand on my shoulder and suggested, "Let's pray together for him." Smiling she quoted, "You know, where two or three are gathered."

There was a little hint of a tear in my eye as I nodded. We slipped into an empty office and prayed.

Not too long after that, I solicited Lucy's prayers again. "I found a lump in my breast. I'm sure it's nothing. No, that's not true. I'm not sure it's nothing, and I'm scared senseless."

Lucy's eyes filled with compassionate tears.

"Then we must pray."

Our empty office now had someone in it, but the picnic area was available.

A few weeks later we prayed together again—this time, prayers of thanksgiving in the women's restroom. God had answered both previous prayers in one fell swoop. My son, so worried that I might have cancer, prayed the prayer of desperation: "I won't touch marijuana again if only Mom is okay." Well, I was okay. The lump was benign. And my son had reached a turning point in his young life, realizing what had value and what did not. God had used my lump as a wake-up call for him.

Prayer became the lynchpin in our relationship. We've prayed in many different and strange places—cars, roadside parks, and even once in a cemetery. When our two families spent time together, our husbands and children came to expect that Nancy and Lucy would want some prayer time together.

When we lived in the same city, we took turns calling each other in the morning to spend a few minutes in prayer before jumping into our busy day. Then I moved and Lucy moved, and daily calls weren't feasible. We kept up with each other through letters and occasional calls and visits, but it wasn't enough. So, we devised a plan of taking turns calling each other on a weekly basis.

Even though we now live 100 miles apart, my prayer partner and I continue to pray. Our families know the Monday night routine, and more than once, we've received requests, "Mom, would you and Lucy (Nancy) pray for—"

> We are unlikely prayer partners. I am Catholic, and Lucy belongs to the Assembly of God church. Although some of the practices of our churches differ, our foundation is the same—Jesus Christ.
>
> —Nancy R. Baker

Before the Throne

Over the years, Lucy and I have prayed our way though illnesses, teenage children, moves, jobs, financial problems, reconciliations, husbands, grandchildren, births, and even deaths. It took six months of solid petition to move my two sons to reconciliation. The hardest and most consistent prayer time we have shared happened when Lucy's husband was stricken with cancer.

"Nancy, Don's sick."

"What's wrong?" I queried, expecting a response like "the flu." Don was 56, a strong man, an outdoors person. He hunted and fished. He was a brick mason by trade and had performed many years as a rodeo clown and a Little League umpire. I could not image anything serious being wrong.

"I don't know," she said, "but he couldn't even stay up for our Thanksgiving celebration."

"Let's pray."

So began many months of prayer for Don. Prayers for strength, for courage, for healing, for doctors, and for answers. Don's condition seesawed: sometimes better, sometimes worse. For the first time in our prayer relationship, Lucy and I included someone else. Don, who was not outwardly a prayerful person, joined us in prayer when I visited. I bought him a teddy bear with angel wings to remind him that I was praying for him. Not to be outdone, he bought me a teddy bear with bunny rabbit ears to remind me to laugh.

Eleven months after being diagnosed, Don went home to be with the Lord. Looking back, Lucy says she could not have survived that year without our prayer time, nor could she have survived the months following. Her heart broke with grief and sadness but she was able to endure, trusting that God keeps His promise to be near the brokenhearted. She took comfort in the fact that Don was safe from all pain and harm and temptation.

This was confirmed for her when, shortly after Don's death, she was at a church service, lifting her voice in song about "worshiping at the throne of God." As she sang the word *throne*, God dropped this image into her mind: She saw Don bowed in praise before God and knew without doubt that she and Don were connected at His throne. Don was praising God at the very same moment that she was. Theirs was not a forever separation, but a temporary one.

It is said that Saint Monica prayed for many years for the conversion of her wayward son. Weary and disheartened, she sought help from her local bishop who encouraged her, "It is not possible the object of so many tears should perish." Her sinner son became her saint son, Augustine.

Lucy and I have shed many tears in prayer. We believe God collects them in His flask and finds them precious, that He hears and answers our prayers.

Nancy R. Baker retired from Texas A&M University in 1999 to pursue her lifelong love of writing. She has been published in *Eucharistic Minister* and *Deacon's Digest* and is a contributing author to *Cup of Comfort for Friends; Cup of Comfort for Women; 911: The Day America Cried;* and *Forget Me Knots.*

Up Close and Personal:

Describe a time when one of your girlfriends showed you the love of Christ. What did she do? How did it impact you?

Legs That Ran

Linda Henson

We both wanted teaching positions. Janice had finally finished college after her third child was kindergarten age, and she was eager to apply her education. I had already taught in Kentucky and Tennessee while my husband finished his seminary training. We had just moved to the small Illinois community where my husband pastored a local church, and we needed the extra salary. Our common goal caused us to meet each Sunday after church to discuss how healthy the present teachers were, who was likely to retire that year, or who might get married and move on.

Janice was a sanguine *par excellence*. She could see the humor in any situation. Her first husband had been an undertaker, and she kept me in stitches with tales of her days in the mortician's home. They had lived upstairs over the mortuary. One day her husband asked her to drive the hearse to pick up a body at the hospital. That was no problem; but as she was driving back through our small town, she forgot about her cargo and the vehicle she was driving. She drove through town, honking the horn, yelling at acquaintances, and stopping to visit. We never had a visit without hysterical laughter.

When I met her, she was faithful in church, but lacked a real relationship with *the* Teacher. However, during our first year at the church, that changed, and we became sisters in our faith. Being a native of the county, she got the first teaching job that opened up. It was part-time, but it was a "foot in the door." After only one semester, a teacher moved and Janice filled the fulltime position. She recommended me for her job, and with that, we were teaching in the same school.

We saw each other every day, and when we had time for visits, we had a new goal: praying for our fellow teachers. That year we saw incredible answers to prayer as we witnessed changed lives. No matter how serious our prayer times, Janice would see something funny, and we would always leave laughing. She made me realize that God surely has a sense of humor. She used her fun-loving personality to attract people to her Source of joy.

Laughter and Log Rides

One summer the youth group in the church planned a trip to an amusement park. Since her daughter was in the group, Janice volunteered to chaperone. I was thrilled. I had no choice—I was the pastor's wife—I had to go. Although we were the "adults" on the trip, I knew we'd still have a ball. It was early in the summer and school hadn't been out long enough for teachers to have tans, so we decided to buy the latest rub-on product and look good in our walking shorts. When we met with the group at 7:00 a.m., we looked like we had been on a Caribbean island. All the teens were amazed that we were darker than them; we didn't give away our secret.

> She made me realize that God surely has a sense of humor. She used her fun-loving personality to attract people to her Source of joy.
>
> —Linda Henson

The bus trip was loud and raucous as any youth trip, but we eventually arrived and made our way through the lines into the area of the rides. Roller coasters were the first choice for the kids, but not for me! I get sick. I sat through a few rounds, and finally they were ready to move on.

"The Log Ride!" screamed one of the kids closest to me.

I know that the log ride is a type of roller coaster, but I decided I could manage it. We wound through the Disney-style lines for nearly an hour until we came in sight of the "logs." Janice and I jumped in the first open seat, which happened to be in the very front. We were off.

At first, it seemed so benign. It chugged along like a little train taking you on a scenic ride; then, the "Little Engine That Could" began his puffing and clanking, pulling his load up the hill. I had just about decided that this ride was a "piece of cake." A black tunnel brought some interest to the ride, but it was nothing that caused heart palpitations.

"This isn't so bad."

I had spoken too soon. Just when I was about to feel comfortable, horror set in. I began to hear sounds of expectation from those behind me on the log.

"Hold on," I heard a dad say to his son.

"Here it comes," squealed one of the teenage girls.

I knew the devilish end to the ride was near, so I braced myself. Sure enough, the light at the end of the tunnel that had seemed so hopeful in the dark, turned out to be a nearly vertical drop. I don't remember anything from that point on except one long scream and then Niagara Falls hitting us square in the face.

We were drenched! But at least we were at the bottom and still in one piece. The log pulled up to the platform, and we began to drip our way to the nearest restroom to try to straighten out the mess. Giggles and out-and-out laughter followed us every step. *What was the matter with those kids? Did we look any worse than the hundreds of other people who had ridden that ride?* Finally, one of the girls cackled, "Look at your legs!" Oh, no! The tan that had been the envy of the day had turned to liquid after the deluge! Great streams of "mud" slid down our legs and pooled on our ankles. Our legs were *running!* We spent the rest of the day looking like we were wearing pantyhose that had walked through a bramble bush. I don't think the teens ever invited us to go anywhere with them after that. We were too embarrassing!

It's hard to find that kind of friend, one who can pray with you and share deep spiritual moments, and also embrace the embarrassing episodes as if each event had been planned so that we'd have great stories to tell for years to come. Friends who remain supportive though miles and years have kept them apart are to be treasured. Today, as a missionary outside of the United States, it's very comforting to know that I still have that friend I can count on who will pray with me or lift my spirits by making me laugh. Recently, when a death in the family occurred, she e-mailed me and offered to fund our trip home. Many years have passed since our legs "ran," and yet, she soon plans to fly here to help us in our mission's work…I'm not sure this country is ready for the two of us!

Linda Henson is a credentialed minister presently serving as a missionary. She writes for a local newspaper and teaches in a Bible college. She is a musician, counselor, speaker for women's conferences, and has taught language arts in the public schools.

Celebrate the Moment:

Make time for your sisters of faith. Call, e-mail, or meet them. Ask them for prayer requests and for praise reports. Begin to chronicle your prayers and how God answers them. As you do, you'll see how faithful He is.

There Is a Friend Who Sticks Closer

Barbara Loftus Boswell

Larissa Okumura was the first born-again Christian that I ever knew, back when the phrase "born again" was synonymous to me with "Bible-thumping zealot."

Not Larissa, though. Hers was a strong, unimposing faith.

We became friends in high school, drawn to one another because of our wacky senses of humor. We'd compose letters to each other in typing class, mine to Larissa O'Kumura, an Irish lass, hers to Sister Babers Angelica, head of an orphanage. To fully understand the irony, you need to know that Larissa is of Japanese descent and that my lifestyle would have certainly prevented my acceptance into any convent!

She and I both chose to study nursing in college and to become roommates. (I can now appreciate the angst her parents must have felt at this decision!) For two years, Larissa modeled her love for God, and for me, while we roomed together. She read her Bible daily, she prayed before meals, and she always tried to be kind to other people. She invited me to Campus Crusade for Christ meetings and included me in many of the activities that she and her Christian friends enjoyed, regardless of the fact that I didn't quite fit in with that crowd.

I, on the other hand, was a pretty selfish, unlovely unbeliever. It amazes me to this day how she put up with me for those two years! She dried my tears and wrote me poems when my heart was breaking over the umpteenth "true-love" that I'd lost. She cleaned me up after a one-too-many-beer-and-Cheez-Whiz combination went awry. She let me drag her along on questionable outings to visit questionable people. She picked me up and called me "friend" when I, time and again, fell flat on my face. She saw something in me that I, at that time, didn't even see in myself—the image of a most-high God.

We had so many crazy, fun times, though! We went on jogs around campus and did "scare-robics" to Lionel Richie and Michael Jackson songs. (If you could've seen us jumping around like madwomen, you'd know why we called them "scarerobics"!) We had an eating contest in the cafeteria, making ourselves thoroughly sick! (Although, as I frequently remind Larissa, I did win by a spoonful of Jell-O!) We cracked ourselves up with our word games and parodies, laughing so loudly at night that other girls on our hallway in the dorm would bang on our door for us to be quiet!

Far and away, the most important thing that Larissa did for me was spending time on her knees for me, praying for my soul.

—Barbara Loftus Boswell

Far and away, the most important thing that Larissa did for me was spending time on her knees for me, praying for my soul.

Now that Jesus is my Lord and Savior, I can see the big part that Larissa played in His plan. Though she and I now live on opposite coasts, we keep in touch by letter and telephone. Larissa laments that she wasn't a more bold witness in our friendship, thinking she might have saved me from some of the pain I inflicted upon myself. I can see, however, that her role was to sow seeds of God's love and grace in my heart.

And by God's extravagant grace and mercy, the seeds she sowed have finally sprouted!

Barbara Loftus Boswell is a fulltime mom of three terrific kids, wife of one great husband, and a parttime writer. She is currently working on a devotional for busy housewives and moms...in between loads of laundry. When she grows up, she wants to be a famous singer.

Precious Seeds

B. Kay Coulter

She came bearing seeds...precious seeds.
Seeds of patience,
Seeds of acceptance,
Seeds of joy,
Seeds of encouragement,
Seeds of hope,
Seeds of affirmation.
These she planted with the labor of love.

Rejoice!

The fruit now is in bloom, and soon to be harvested.
Her friend receives the first fruits, and then—
They walk hand in hand together to bring in the sheaves:
The fruits produced in others' lives—
Because of One who planted seeds of love in both.

B. Kay Coulter is one-half of Lovebound Ministries, a partnership ministry with Janet Crews. Kay is a vocalist, speaker, and the author of *Proverbs for Personalities* and *Victim/Victor: It's Your Choice.* She is a wife, mother, and grandmother and lives in Temple, Texas.

Cup of Tea and Prayer Sister

Katherine Murphy

"Come in, come in." She'd greet me at the door with a big hug. "Shall we start with some tea?"

"Of course," I'd say, and we'd boil water, drink tea, warm and soothing, settle in an overstuffed chair, and catch up on the past week. From there, our conversation inevitably turned to our children and their friends. We spoke of the varied and negative influences that pulled our children away from us. We shared scriptures that touched us, spiritual books we were reading, and prayers that brought us comfort. I always left our times together feeling lighthearted and peaceful, no matter what was going on in my life.

I hadn't always prayed for my children, but as my children grew through their teens, there were trying times that brought me to my knees. I knew the most important thing I could do for them was pray. I remember talking with my friend Maureen one day and discovering that she, with children the same age, felt the same way. That's what prompted us to get together and pray for our children.

Going Public

After meeting like this for a couple of years, Maureen and I were convinced there were other mothers who would benefit, as we did, by joining together in prayer. Thus, we decided to move our little group into the church. I would never have done this on my own, but with Maureen's support and that of our pastor, she and I started a Mothers' Prayer Group.

Using Lent as a focus, we began on Ash Wednesday a number of years ago. Not knowing what to expect, we were pleasantly surprised when a dozen or more mothers showed up that first day. Since then, every Wednesday morning, mothers and grandmothers meet at our church's chapel for the hour-long meeting.

Each week our group begins with a recitation of "A Mother's Prayer." Maureen leads us in the Act of Contrition and then a time of thanksgiving follows. One woman might share a scripture. Another, an event of the week that demonstrates God's presence. Still another woman might mention a current event—the most recent, the war in Iraq.

One after another, women add what they are thankful for in their children's lives.

"My daughter and I did not have a fight this morning about her going to school."

"My son was out late with friends Saturday night and came home safely."

"Doctors are beginning to find answers to my son's health problems."

"My granddaughter came up with an idea for her school project and was able to follow through with it."

Then we recite the rosary for our children and the intentions placed in our petition box, and close our hour with a few short prayers. Each one of us leaves encouraged and ready to meet the day's challenges, keeping our children and all young people in prayer—for we have shared with God and one another the blessed vocation of motherhood.

Over the years, I have grown close and feel a special connection to these women. Some have returned to work and can no longer attend. Yet, whenever I meet one of them at the supermarket deli counter or somewhere else in town, I always exchange a hug, and we talk about what's new in our lives. We're connected.

My Special Gift

But, of course, for my friend Maureen, my cup of tea and prayer sister, the praying does not stop there. Over the years there have been many times when I have called her with an urgent request involving one of my children or she has done likewise. There have been times when I have called just to chat and discovered in our talking that I needed prayer. No matter the time of day or the reason, she has always been there for me—a sister to pray with and through whom to feel the Lord's peace. A sister who has encouraged me to grow, step out, and lead a group of other mothers in prayer.

Truly, she is a sister given to me from God; we are bonded as if by blood and birth through the special gift of prayer.

A Mother's Prayer

Dear God, we come before You today, bringing our children, their needs, and our concerns for them. But first, we give thanks to You, O God, for You are our Lord, our Creator, and our Maker, from whom all good things come.

Thank You, God, for the gift of our children. You alone know how important they are to us, how much we want what is best for them, and how much their lives are woven into the very heart and fabric of our own. Yet in spite of this, we know that they are gifts from You, given to us for a time. They are not ours to keep or control, nor are they our possessions. As much as we sometimes think this and try to mold them according to our wants and desires, we know it is only Your will for them that matters. It is Your plan for their lives we are required to advance.

So we come before You, O God, to appeal for Your blessings. We ask You to show us the way. Lead us with Your light down the path You have paved for our children. Strengthen us so that we can love and nurture them in Your ways. Help us to be both the mothers You would have us be and the mothers our children need. Fill us with Your knowledge that we might understand the way of the world today and understand how changed it is from our youth. Stand in that gap where our world cannot intersect with theirs, in that void where our generation cannot touch theirs. Instill in us the courage to stand firm against the powers of the world that await, often unrecognizable to us, ready to snatch our children away from us, away from You.

We ask, too, O God, for Your grace in all decisions we make for our children. Impart Your wisdom upon us when things for them do not go the way we would like, when things seem instead to get worse. Grant us Your patience to understand that Your ways are not our ways, that Your time is not our time. Bestow on us Your comfort that we might know we are always acting in Your stead, that all things will work out for the best for our children because they are first and foremost Your children.

We petition, O heavenly Father, for Your loving protection upon our children. We ask that You travel through each day with them, to all the places where they go and we do not, for You are Father to us all, our Rock, our Strength, the Salvation of our world. We ask these things in the name of Your Son, our Lord Jesus Christ. Amen.

Katherine Murphy's essays and poetry have appeared in many publications, including *A Time of Singing; Kalliope; Key West: A Collection; Family Digest; St. Anthony Messenger; Word among Us*; and aired over NPR. Her memoir, *Awake O Sleeper: How I Rediscovered God through Breast Cancer* was published in October of 2003.

Intimate Details:

We take our lead from Christ, who is the source of everything we do. He keeps us in step with each other. His very breath and blood flow through us, nourishing us so that we will grow up healthy in God, robust in love.

Ephesians 4:15–16 MSG

Inspirational Insight:

"Carry each other's burdens." Those are strong words. They remind us that God wants us to be involved in each other's lives.

When you think of a time that a friend has helped you through a difficult time—a divorce, a loss, a change—could you have imagined facing it without her? Can you imagine how things would have been different if she hadn't supported you?

Today, it's common to walk by people who are hurting, to refuse to get involved, but God wants us to be involved. He wants us to have sisters of faith who will pray for our children, hold our hands through the tragedies, and make us laugh at ourselves. He wants us to celebrate their lives and allow them to celebrate ours. As we do, we will continue to "grow up healthy in God" and fulfill His plan for the body of Christ.

Heart to Heaven:

Lord, thank You for the Sisters of Faith you've sent into my life. Help me to honor and support them as they do me. And as we honor each other, may all we do honor You. Amen.

Chapter Twelve

FOREVER FRIENDS:

Growing Up Together

A man of many companions may come to ruin, but there is a friend who sticks closer than a brother.

Proverbs 18:24

I once read a poster that said: "Good friends are like stars—you don't always see them, but you always know they are there." I like that—especially because it perfectly describes my friendships with Angie and Raegan.

Angie and I became friends on the first day of kindergarten. A little unsure of how to make friends, I asked my mother how to meet other children on that first day of school. She suggested I go up to another little girl and simply say, "Hi. My name is Missy (my nickname) Medlock. Would you be my friend?" Sounded good to me, so I gave it a shot.

I saw Angie Massette across the room. I eyeballed her all during milk break, and then I marched right over to her and uttered: "Hi. My name is Missy Medlock. Would you be my friend?"

Angie looked at me as if I'd lost my ever-loving mind. Still, she must have taken pity on the little girl with pigtails that were too tight and a faint, red Kool-Aid mustache, because she answered, "Sure."

The rest, as they say, is history. We became best friends that day, and we've been best friends ever since. Sure, we've had other buddies over the years, but the two of us were inseparable—joined at the hip. There wasn't room for any other close friends—until we met Raegan Holiday in the fourth grade.

Angie and I lived in the same neighborhood and rode our Huffy bikes all over the addition all summer long. As hot and humid as Indiana summers are, we longed for a swimming pool. Neither of us had one—unless you count the plastic frog-shaped one that sat in my side yard. Then, Raegan moved into the addition. And, she moved into the house on the corner with a SWIMMING POOL!

We weren't sure how to meet this new little girl, but just like Lucy and Ethel, Angie and I came up with a brilliant plan. We put on our bathing suits, draped our beach towels around our necks, and strapped on our goggles. Then, we rode our bikes over to Raegan's house and hung out by the street corner saying clever things like, "Whew! It's sure hot out here. Wish there was some place we could swim."

Raegan's mother, Patsy, must have admired our gustiness and invited us in one afternoon. We soon discovered that we liked Raegan for much more than her pool. She was a cool kid—who had even won a tiara in a beauty pageant. I was sure it was made of real diamonds.

The Terrific Twosome became the Three Musketeers, and it's been that way ever since. Through dance recitals, cheer camps, fad diets, fashion fiascos, triple dates, proms, heartbreaks, broken engagements, Spring Break vacations, SATs, college courses, marriages, births, miscarriages, cross-country moves, and everything else in life, we've been there for one another—forever friends.

Some friends are fair-weathered. Some friends are only for a season. Others are friends due to circumstances. But few friends are friends forever. Those friends are worth more than jewels—even diamond tiaras. Those forever-kind-of-friends are the ones we celebrate in this chapter. Friends come and friends go, but Angie and Raegan will always be in my life—just like the stars. Here's hoping you have some stars in your life, too! *MMA*

Forever Friends and Fairytales

Stacy Smith

We lay on our backs in my backyard, gazing at the countless stars that hung over us from a sky that seemed just beyond our grasp. A cricket chirped, and a cool summer night's breeze wafted across our faces as we pulled our sleeping bags up to our chins.

"What will we do when we grow up?" Christi wondered wistfully.

"We'll definitely be best friends," I stated, not wanting to think of where we could be in ten years.

"We have to go to college together and be roomies," she said.

"And marry two guys that are best friends, too," I added.

"We'll be in each other's weddings…maids of honor."

"We'll live next door to each other and ride horses all the time. And have white picket fences and matching yellow labs!" I added, laughing.

Christi giggled at the thought of it all.

"And," she almost whispered, still smiling but her voice carrying a more somber tone, "our daughters will be best friends, too."

I realized, just as she did, that we were merely dreaming, and that in reality we would probably lose touch sooner or later. Even if, at the time, it seemed incomprehensible to my thirteen-year-old mind that my best friend would ever not be a part of my life. I wanted the fairytale. I wanted the "happily-ever-after" ending for both of us, and I wanted us to be best friends forever. I rolled over in my disco-blue sleeping bag and hugged her. Without saying anything more, we watched the twinkling night sky, lost in our own thoughts about the future, and fell asleep before the hot morning sun woke us up to start another summer day.

Hospital Gowns and Goodbyes

That was only five months before I found myself standing at the foot of her hospital bed, trying to comprehend that my best friend was dying of leukemia.

I had been in school that day, on my way to my final class, when I heard my name paged over the loudspeaker. "Stacy Smith, please come to the principal's office immediately." I knew I wasn't in trouble. The past few weeks I had not had enough energy, enough zest for life, to be in any kind of trouble. I carried the constant weight on my shoulders that I was in school, in the "outside world" living life, and my best friend was confined to a bed in a hospital. It had only been a few weeks since that fateful call that rocked the foundation of my world. *The doctors think I have leukemia.* The past month had been a blur, as I roamed through the halls of my life like a zombie on autopilot. I had been to see her a couple of times at first, but lately they said she wasn't allowed to have visitors because her immune system was too weak.

With a heavy sense of dread, I went to the principal's office, and there were my parents. My mom was crying, and Dad looked pale and solemn.

"The doctors think you should come see Christi," he said softly. I looked at them, my eyes full of questions.

"They…they aren't sure she'll make it through the night."

The realization sunk to my stomach like a slowly sinking brick … *They want me to say goodbye.*

I felt like a mannequin, hardened and numb and empty as they dressed me, draped me in blue hospital robes and gloves, and placed a blue mask over my mouth and nose so that I couldn't pass any of my germs to her and kill her. The sterile smell of the hospital made me ill. Or, was it the fact that I was about to go in and see my best friend for what could be the last time?

The doctor gave me strict instructions to not touch her and to talk about my everyday life, anything but her sickness. "Don't let her know that we think she's declining," he added.

How could I tell her about things I had been doing, while she was trapped in this morbid hospital room? How could I tell her about movies and friends and homework? How could I pretend nothing was wrong, when my favorite friend in the world was on the verge of death?

I saw the concern in her parents' eyes, expressionless above their blue-masked mouths. I knew they were frowning, maybe biting their lips to keep from crying. Taking a deep breath, the nurse opened her door for me since they didn't even want me to touch the sterilized silver door handle. And then it closed, and I was there with a stranger. She looked like one, anyway. I was suddenly glad for the mask because I knew my mouth had dropped open at the sight of her frail body. I looked at this person whom the doctors claimed was Christi, my best friend. But I knew there had to be a mistake. This fragile skeleton could not be the shell of the person who had become as much a part of my life as my own beating heart and the oxygen that I breathed.

She smiled weakly, and I sat near her bedside, not allowing myself to touch her. I stared out the window and saw the hints of a sunset reflecting off the dirty building next door. This was her life now. All those needles in her waiflike arms, and the machines hooked up to her bony body...it was all too surreal. I couldn't grasp that it was happening. And I couldn't accept the fact that, for the first time since we'd met three years ago, I couldn't find the words to say to my best friend.

She was my soul mate; the one who finished my sentences before me, who could burst out laughing from just a shared glance. We knew each other's thoughts before we could think them. My dad called us "Tweedledum and Tweedledee," because where you saw one of us, the other one was surely nearby creating some incident to make us laugh. We truly had the kind of friendship that they make movies about. We shared records, clothes, our biggest dreams, and our deepest fears. We went to our first concert together, our first day of junior high together, and bought our first bras together. We were there to support each other through our first periods, our first loves, and our first broken hearts. So, how could we suddenly be a world apart, seemingly so separated in this small room?

We made small talk, my heart fighting to ignore the doctor's orders. I wanted to scream. I wanted to ask her questions. Does it hurt? Are you scared? A nurse knocked lightly before popping her head in.

"I think Christi needs her rest now," she said before quietly closing the door. *No,* I thought. *Please. Please don't make this be our last moment.* I looked at Christi, and she smiled.

"Like I need more rest," she whispered weakly. We both laughed a little, and I felt all the discomfort melt away. Under the alien disguise, she was still my best friend. I let the tears come and then stood as she reached out her hand to mine.

"They said I can't touch you," I whispered, trying to hold back my impending sobs.

"I don't care," she whispered back, her large brown eyes sad above her small smile. I laughed as my tears flowed. *Forget their dumb rules,* I thought. *They think she is going to die anyway. I want her to remember my hug, no matter what happens.*

"*There's* my rebellious friend," I joked as I leaned down and gently wrapped my arms around her tiny, delicate body. I paused, letting all my energy pour into her soul, saying a quick prayer, and imagining Jesus working His miracles through me and making her all better.

I pulled myself away and stood at the door.

"I'll see you in a few days," I said, my heart positively breaking at the knowledge that that might not be true. I then went outside and looked blankly at her parents and the doctors, then shuffled numbly down the hall to cry my soul dry.

Prayers, Posters, and Promises

The next morning Christi's mom called us. She'd made it through the night. We were on our way to church, and that morning we asked our church to pray for her. I sat there and looked at the hundreds of bowed heads while the pastor prayed for my best friend. A small part of me was angry because they would never know the girl they were praying for. That night, I stole downstairs while my parents slept. In the quiet darkness I dialed the number for a prayer chain I had seen in the church bulletin. My heart pounding, my voice quivering, I told the lady on the other end of the phone that I needed help in praying for my best friend who was fighting for her life. The lady on the phone cried with me while we prayed. I think this was the first moment I truly understood what people meant when they said they turned to God for strength.

That week, the doctors said she was well enough that I could visit again. My mom and I went out and bought brightly colored, positive, spiritual posters and plastered them on her walls. Christi had not been raised in a "churchgoing" environment, and a small part of me worried that she or her parents would be angry at our subtle efforts. But we found our strength in God, and felt that perhaps she could too.

She continued to amaze the doctors as she grew stronger each day. She continued to defy all logic as her tests came back more positive each time. And we continued to pray and shower her with positive thoughts and subtle talk about God. Six months later, Christi left the hospital and came home. The doctors called her a "miracle case." Five years later, she was considered in remission, and now, twenty years later, she is considered cured.

Through the grace of God and His healing hand, Christi and I were able to fulfill almost all of the promises we had made on that summer night under the stars. We graduated high school together, and we actually did go to college and live together as roommates. I stood at her side as her maid of honor at her wedding, and someday if I get married, she will be mine. She has an amazing husband and three healthy, beautiful children, and I bear the proud title of godmother to her firstborn son. She and her husband share a strong faith in the Lord and are raising their children to know and love Jesus.

I am not sure when she began to believe in God. I wonder if it was during her sickness, if that is when she felt Him the most. I look at her children and wonder if they'll ever realize how close they came to never "being," how close we all came to losing their mother years before. I wonder if they will ever comprehend what a true gift the miracle of life is, and how each and every person you love should be treasured. Someday they might understand. But for now, it's enough to see Christi in their eyes and in their smiles, hear her laugh in their laughter, and know that with enough faith, forever friends and fairytales can come true.

Stacy Smith is a freelance writer from her home in the mountains of Colorado. She travels the world extensively and writes for corporations and small businesses, and is also working on several books and screenplays. She and Christi still consider each other their "forever best friend."

Heart to Heart:

Do you have a forever-kind-of-friend in your life? If so, describe her—what makes her so special?

Is there a friend you've lost touch with—a friend that you once thought would be a forever friend? Why did you lose communication? Wouldn't you like to reconnect?

God's Pair

Michelle Medlock Adams

A special friend is hard to find
That's why I treasure you
We have a special kind of bond
That only best friends do.

You challenge me to push myself
And reach for every star
You're always there to cheer me on
'Cause that's the way you are.

You're caring and you're genuine
You're special as can be
You look past all my shortcomings
And help me laugh at me.

I know that I am very blessed
To have a friend like you
You make me feel so special by
The little things you do.

Our friendship's not by accident
God paired us up this way
That's why our friendship will remain
Forever and a day.

Michelle Medlock Adams holds a journalism degree from Indiana University and a passion for writing in her heart. An award-winning journalist, she has received top honors from the Associated Press and the Society of Professional Journalists. She is the author of 22 books, including *Why I Love You, God* and *Memories of the Manger.* She is also a popular speaker at women's conferences and writers' conferences around the country. She is married to her high school sweetheart, Jeff, and they have two daughters, Abby and Allyson.

Up Close and Personal:

Record five significant moments in your life (marriage, births, deaths, etc.). Now, write what your forever friend did for you during each of those events. Maybe she served as your maid of honor in your wedding. Maybe she held your hand during a catastrophic time. Maybe she watched your children for you. Maybe she just made you laugh at yourself. Now, write about how different those times would have been if your forever friend hadn't been there for you.

Best Friends and Bathroom Stalls

Shannon Kubiak

It was my first night in my new dorm building. I was a freshman in college, and I had no clue what I was doing. My parents had just pulled away; my roommate hadn't arrived yet; and I was biting a hole through my bottom lip in an attempt to keep from crying. I wrote in my journal and flipped through the pages of a book, trying to distract myself from the emotions that welled up inside of me. Finally I decided that it was time to go to bed.

I grabbed my new shower caddy and headed toward the communal bathroom. As an only child, I'd never shared a room or a bathroom before. I was okay with having one roommate; it was the thirty bathroom mates that worried me. Cautiously, I pushed the cold metal door open and peered into the bathroom. At first it appeared as if no one else was there, so I entered.

As I began to unload my stuff onto the sink counter, I heard a noise that sounded like crying. As I lathered my face with soap, the sound grew louder. As I rinsed my face, I heard the door to one of the bathroom stalls open, and there stood a girl with tears streaming down her face. She looked miserable.

With my face still dripping wet, and soap stinging my eyes, I squinted at her and cautiously asked, "Are you all right?"

She hesitated before she spoke, then she introduced herself as Rebecca. "I just started my period, and my boxes with all of my stuff in them haven't arrived yet, and there aren't even any machines in these bathrooms," she said.

"I can help you with that," I offered, thinking of the boxes and boxes full of things my mom had lovingly packed for me. "Come with me," I said, bounding down the hall and drying my face at the same time.

Rebecca followed. When we got to my room, I raided my supplies and loaded her up with enough stuff to last her until her own boxes arrived.

We said our good-byes that night, each feeling a little bit better about our new life at college. It was a reminder that this stuff was new to all of us, and we could all adjust together.

Although it didn't happen right away, we eventually became the best of friends. Rebecca became part of the core group that would help me survive both the trials and triumphs of college. Together we celebrated birthdays, the end of finals, and every holiday known to man—sometimes we even made up our own. We took trips, watched movies, and stayed up all night sharing our secret dreams and deepest desires. We went on dates we regretted, and made scrapbooks full of so many memories that you had to sit on them to get them closed. We even became roommates our senior year.

Rebecca and I also shared heartaches. In college, we lost grandparents, got homesick, and questioned our callings in life. We had classes we hated, got frustrated with a constant lack of privacy, and sometimes we even got the awful stomach flu. But life, whatever it brought with it, bonded us, and we spent summers and school breaks racking up high phone bills and taking advantage of e-mail so we could keep in touch.

We were each other's sounding board, saving grace, and biggest fan. We were lifelong friends who had met in a public bathroom when one of us needed a tampon. I've learned a million lessons from Rebecca over the years, and I am so thankful to God that we met. To me, Rebecca is evidence that God is always at work. Her friendship has taught me to look for the divine in the mundane, and to always offer what I can to those around me.

After all, on our first night of college, I thought I was just giving a random girl a box of tampons, but God knew I was making a forever friend.

Shannon Kubiak is the author of *The Divine Dance*, a book for young women on how to live for the Lord instead of performing for the world. She has a passion for God and a passion for encouraging women to know Him better. She has a BA in Journalism from Biola University.

The Pleasure of Friendship

Lisa White

"Hello," I spoke into the receiver—only to hear a very familiar voice on the other end. "I can't believe it's you!"

I was delighted to hear from my best friend from high school. It had been more than ten years since I had seen her or spoken to her. Memories started flooding my mind as I listened to her voice.

We had been inseparable in high school, and 2002 marked the eighteenth year since we had last walked those school hallways. We had been through all of the usual teenage milestones together—from crushes on the cutest boy that week to the death of my grandmother when I was fifteen. She had been the first one I called, and she had come to comfort me without question or hesitation.

"Sure, I'll go if you'll go," I answered. "A class reunion sounds like fun."

In April 2002, we attended a reunion for our year—The Class of '84. That night reopened a part of my life that I thought had been lost forever. That night brought my best friend back into my life.

With regular e-mails and telephone calls between the two of us, the rest of 2002 swept by. We even booked a holiday together in Scotland, and we took our families away and enjoyed a great week together. By this time, my friend and my brother had become an item. It truly felt like a family holiday. It had been twenty years since we had shared a holiday together. She commented that it felt like coming home—that's how close she is to my family and me.

On Christmas Day, we celebrated together. Then, we all came together to ring in the New Year. As we laughed and danced (to all the great '80s tracks), we were transported back to that decade. Time and distance had not worn away our special friendship. It was at that moment I realized that true friends are there even when there are obstacles to overcome or miles to separate them. That's one of friendship's simple pleasures.

When you can mention someone's name that only the two of you remember and you collapse into a fit of giggles—that is friendship. When you can be made to feel like a teenager again, every now and then—that is friendship. When you can be in a room with your friend and not say anything and it feels natural—that indeed is a simple pleasure.

> Time and distance had not worn away our special friendship. It was at that moment I realized that true friends are there even when there are obstacles to overcome or miles to separate them. That's one of friendship's simple pleasures.
>
> —Lisa White

In February of this year, my other grandmother died, and again, my friend was there to comfort me in my hour of need. Whatever life throws at me, I know she will be there. She is always just a call, text message, or e-mail away. There is no excuse now for us to ever be apart from each other. The friendship we have has endured almost twenty-four years, and even though we don't see each other every day, in our hearts we are together.

Who knows what the future will bring? We may end up as sisters-in-law at some point, and I can't think of anyone else I would like my brother to share his life with. She is already part of my family, and I intend to keep it that way.

I'm glad the telephone rang and catapulted my best friend back into my life. Our high-school class reunion reunited our two hearts, and I am so grateful.

Lisa White is thirty-five years old and lives in Halesowen, England. She is currently completing a writing course. She enjoys writing humor, especially about everyday life, and she has had viewpoint articles, humor pieces, and a short travel article published.

Emily Rider–Longmaid is thirteen years old and lives in Massachusetts with her parents and brother. She likes to write and has had a short story accepted for publication. She has won several academic awards. Emily is an avid soccer and basketball player and plays for her town's traveling teams. She loves science and spending time with friends.

Celebrate the Moment:

Instead of buying a birthday gift for your forever friend this year, why not start now and create something really special for her? Make a scrapbook, filled with special photos and memories of fun times spent together. Or, if you're poetically inclined, write a poem about what she really means to you and have it professionally framed. Or, maybe you could dedicate a song to her as a long-distance dedication on one of those Top 40 shows. The possibilities are endless. Show her how much you care—and if you don't want to wait until her birthday, that's okay, too!

Intimate Details:

Do not forsake your friend and the friend of your father.

Proverbs 27:10

Inspirational Insight:

Deep in the Hundred Acre woods, Pooh Bear leaned over and whispered to Piglet, "We will be friends until forever, just you wait and see."

I love that quote. Every time I think about Pooh's words, I have to smile.

"Until forever" is a long, long time, and that's the kind of friendship that is very hard to find—unless, of course, you live in the Hundred Acre Woods.

Maybe you don't have a forever friend in your life right now—but you can. Jesus wants to be your forever friend. He will walk beside you through the good and the bad. The Bible tells us that He is a Friend who sticks closer than a brother.

He's a forever Friend.

If You haven't asked Jesus to be the Lord of your life, we can take care of that right now. Pray this simple prayer: "Lord, I admit that I have sinned and that I need You in my life. I ask that You come and abide in me today and forevermore. Thank You for forgiving my sins and cleansing me from all unrighteousness. Thank You for being my forever Friend. Amen."

Heart to Heaven:

Heavenly Father, I want to thank You for my forever friends. I can't imagine life without them. You must love me an awful lot to place such amazing women in my life. I am so grateful, Lord. I am also thankful that You are my forever Friend. I know that You will never leave me or forsake me because You promise that in Your Word. I praise You for that. Lord, help me to be a faithful friend—just like You. I love You, Amen.

ABOUT THE AUTHORS

Michelle Medlock Adams

After graduating with a journalism degree from Indiana University, **Michelle Medlock Adams** landed her first job as a city government reporter for "The Bedford Times-Mail" in Southern Indiana. During her time at the paper, Michelle earned many awards from the Associated Press, the Society of Professional Journalists, the Hoosier State Press Association and the American Association of Sunday and Feature Editors.

Today, Michelle enjoys a fulltime writing career, crafting articles for magazines, newspapers, websites and a worldwide ministry. She is the author of 22 books, including her award-winning picture book, *Conversations On The Ark*. In addition, Michelle speaks at women's retreats, churches, schools, colleges and writers' conferences. Michelle is married to her high school sweetheart, Jeff, and they have two "tween-age" daughters, Abby Leigh and Allyson Michelle.

Gena Maselli

The heart of **Gena Maselli's** writing is to encourage others in the plans God has for their lives. She has written several books, including *Truth Unplugged for Girls, Truth Unplugged for Guys* and *Daily Wisdom for Working Women*—a 365-day devotional co-authored with Michelle Medlock Adams. Gena also writes magazine articles, curriculum and marketing materials, and she writes for some of the most effective ministers of our time.

She lives in Fort Worth, Texas, with her husband, children's author Christopher Maselli, and their beautiful baby girl. In her free time—something she has very little of since her daughter was born—Gena enjoys trying out new recipes in her kitchen, taking walks with her family, and laughing with her close friends.